strange vintage fictions

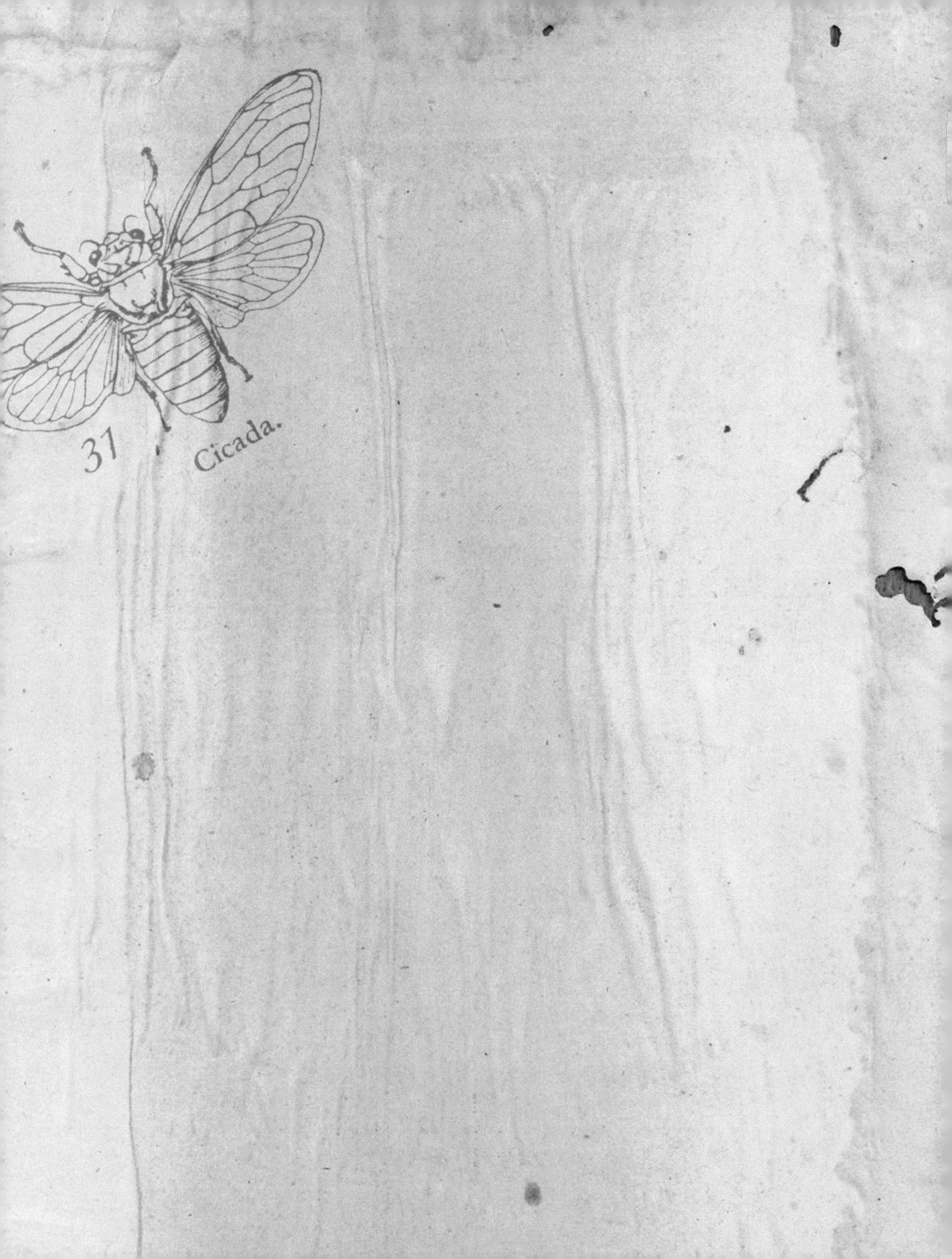

31　　Cicada.

Strange Vintage Fictions

Julie Miller

L.T. Godsmith Press

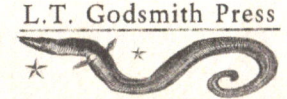

Strange Vintage Fictions

ISBN- 978-0-9838212-4-3

First edition: September 2011
L.T. Godsmith Press

www.haggisvitae.com
E-mail: haggisvitae@gmail.com

Printed in the U.S.A.

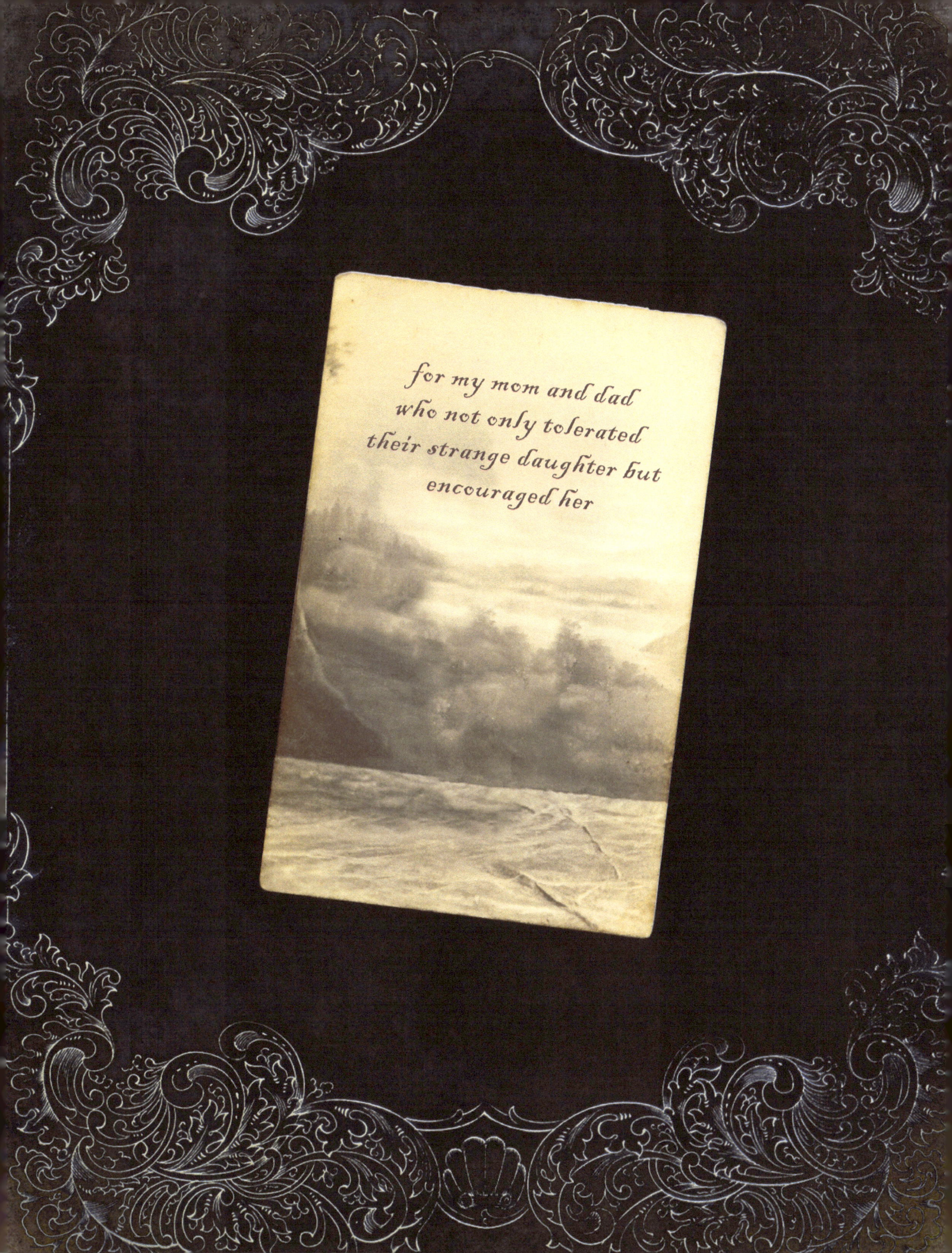

for my mom and dad
who not only tolerated
their strange daughter but
encouraged her

Strange Vintage Fictions?

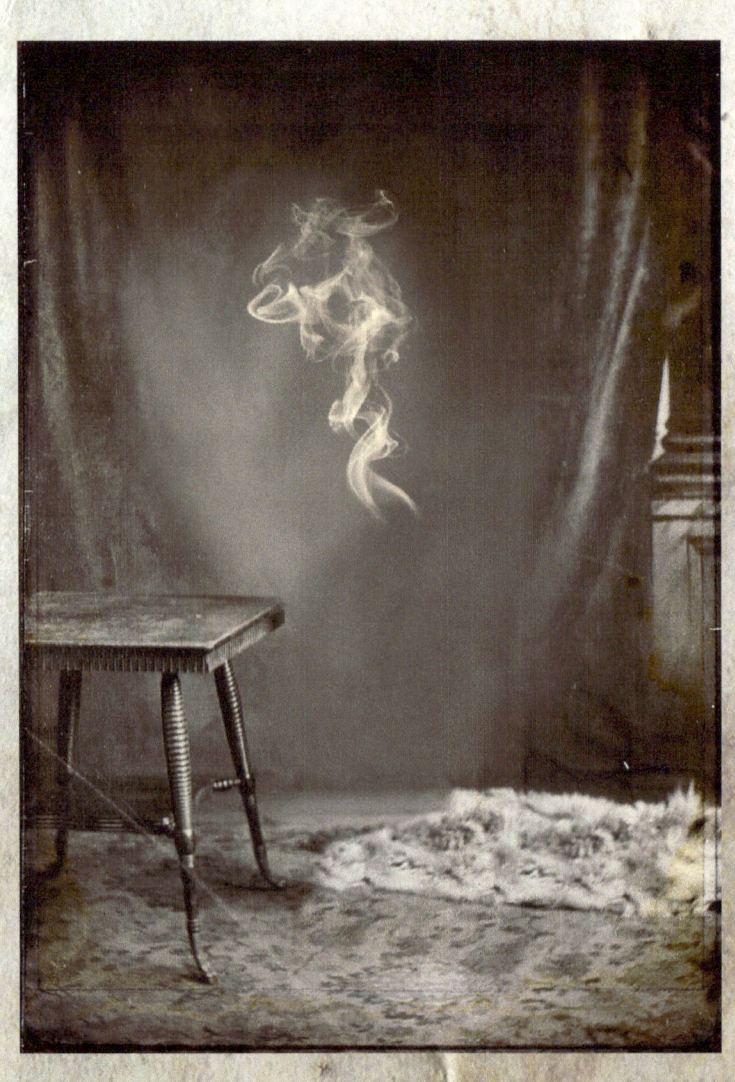

What am I getting into? You may be asking yourself. *Who is HaggisVitae and what's a Strange Vintage Fiction?* Put your mind at ease, pour a cup of tea, and read on.

A few years back, I began gravitating away from paintbrush and canvas towards a more digital surrealism. What I found out there, in the way of digital artwork, was lots and lots of very slick, shiny graphics that said—*there's no other explanation, I've been created by a computer*. This is not what I wanted. Instead, it was my desire to create images using photoshop that didn't have the feel of polished, super-saturated, perfect graphics, but of real paper and texture and age. So I began play around with old photos. I started a flickr account, created the user name HaggisVitae, and began uploading. What I found was a small group of like-minded artists and writers who added stories and comments under my images. They inspired me and supported me and continue to do so. And HaggisVitae? Well, she became my alter ego of sorts, my on-line artist persona responsible for these odd creations. And so *Strange Vintage Fictions* and *HaggisVitae* were born.

Most of all I want to cause the viewer to stop and wonder how such an odd image could exist and yet somehow contain a kernel of truth. What is happening? How is it possible? Where did these old images of magic and mayhem come from? I want them to appear seamless, to not have the look of a collage where pieces and parts are obviously pasted and taped together—my own brand of magical realism. With digital image-making software and a digital draw pad and pen, an entire universe opened up for me. The craziest of stories was now possible. Anything was possible. If I could describe my images, I'd say: think of putting the work of Tim Burton, Edward Gorey, The Brothers Quay, Charles Dickens, E.A. Poe and Terry Gilliam into a blender—and something totally new survives. Then imagine filtering this ghostly concoction through a rusty sieve. These small particulates are my vintage fictions. And to all these artists I owe so very much.

All of my images tell a story—some I create for you and others I ask you to create for yourself. It's my hope that you'll laugh most of the time, be perplexed some of the time, and maybe mildly frightened just a bit. Mostly, find joy in my warped and happy universe where science and art collide, where the might-have-been is dusty, mildewed and yellowed with age, where strange characters feel comfortably at home, where bugs are beautiful, where the past dwells in your oddest dreams and mildest nightmares.

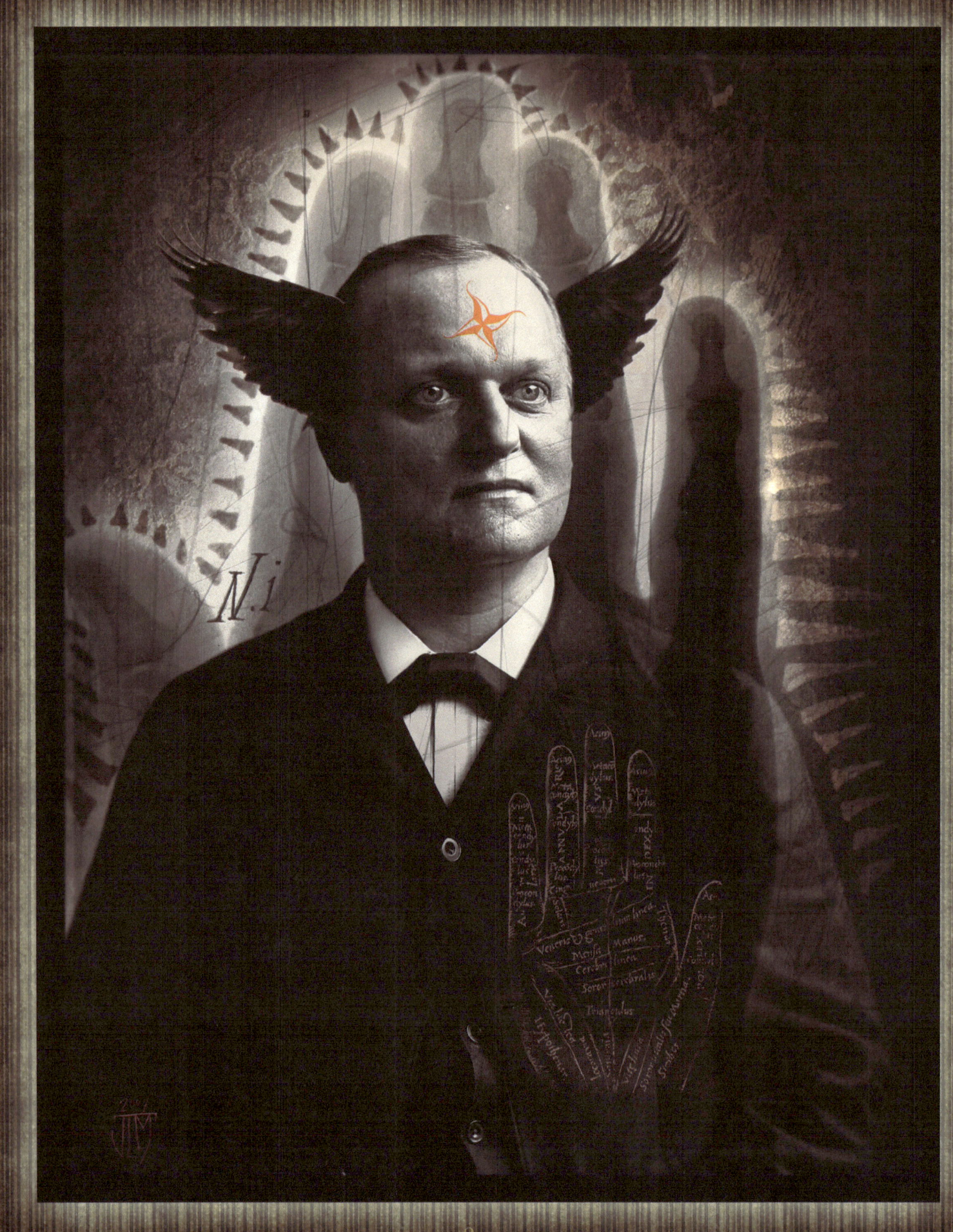

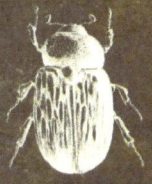

His Holiness
The Bahbra Binki

In this his only formal portrait, Bahbra Binki, renowned Sufi master and dervish with the most consecutive gold metals in whirling, is seen here in full regalia and looking pensive. When pressed for the meanings of the symbols within the portrait, Binki swore it was standard fare for a dervish of his rank, looked around nervously, coughed in a violent manner and begged for a lozenge. Soon after this photo was taken he was said to have run off with a massive leather-clad man who went by the name of Simkins—a strange character himself, purported to have kept a small "humanoid" companion on a leash which screamed, 'gimme some!' unmercifully. Binki was also the author of the acclaimed book of Haiku entitled, *I Have Something in My Third Eye.*

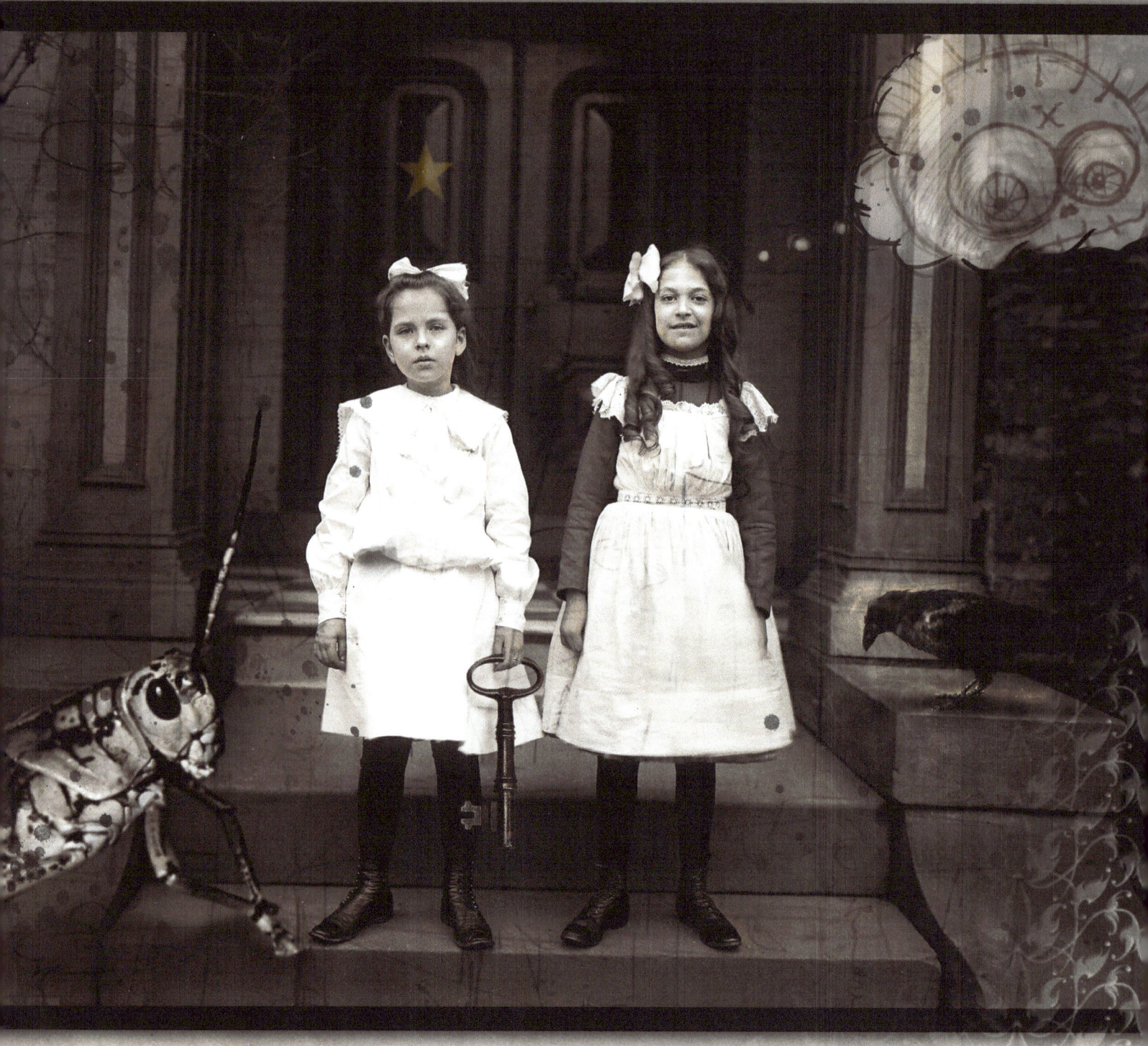

The Harshound Sisters

Elegia and Epithia Harshound were sisters, at least in name, though their genetics differed to an extent unbeknownst to all save Mrs. Harshound. Luckily for her, DNA was still but a mystery, and her secret remained safe. While Elegia was the golden child—smart, beautiful and talented though tragically stoic and unable to smile, Epithia was the dreamer, possessing a most creative mind as well as the ability to find joy everywhere. They are seen here with accompanying spirit animals—for Elegia, a giant grasshopper named Gareth, and for Epitheia, a beautiful black crow she called Drear.

10

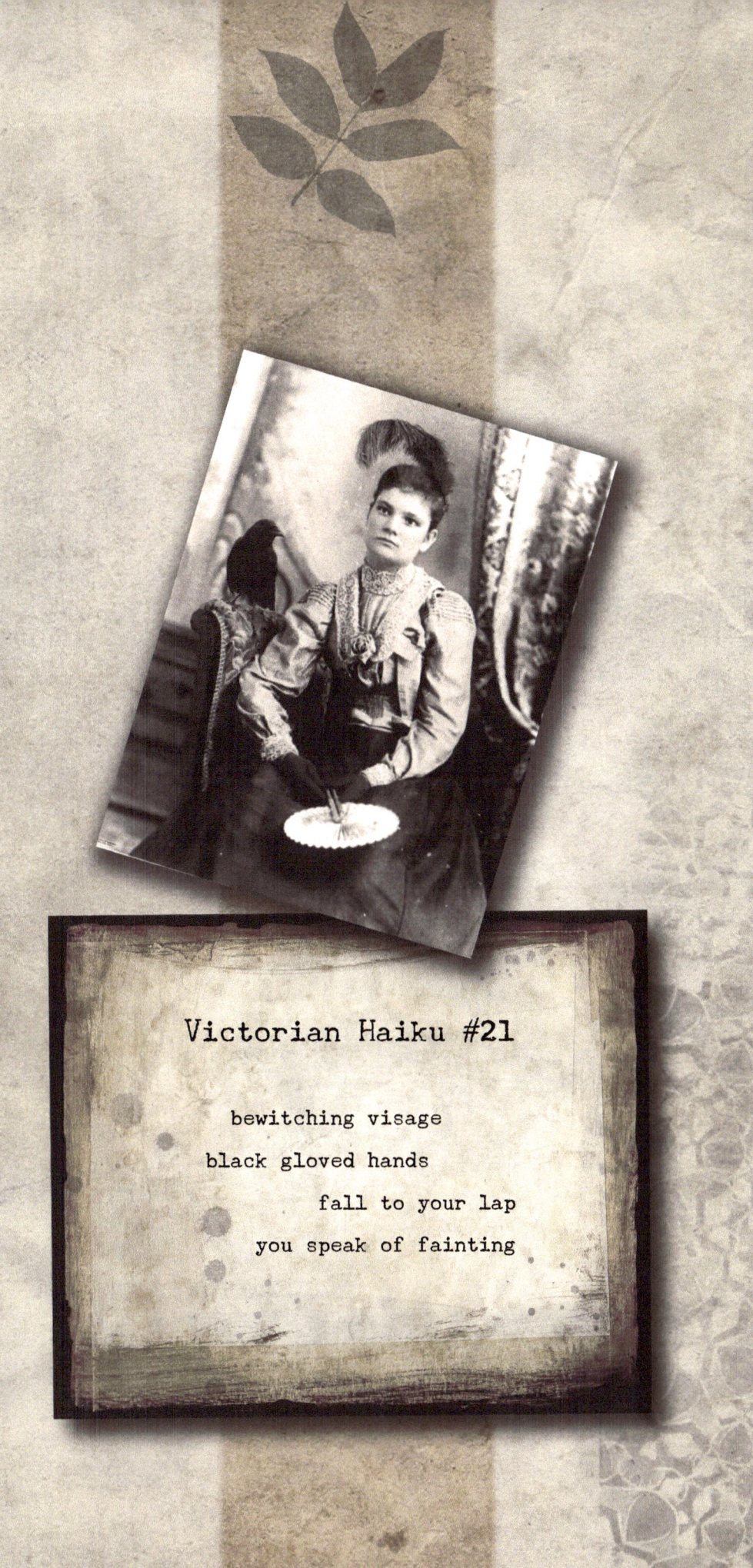

Victorian Haiku #21

bewitching visage
black gloved hands
fall to your lap
you speak of fainting

PRUDENCE FENWICK AND FRIENDS

Prudence fancied herself a sort of St. Francis figure, bringing love and kindness to all animals and keeping a special few with her at all times. There was Jeff the dog of uncertain origin who refused to let his front paws touch the ground, believing himself to be more highly evolved than all other canines. Prudence also kept a crow whom she named Moribund. Unfortunately, Moribund took to staring tirelessly at Jeff, causing him much grief and a painful rash. They are seen here in the darkly charming Fenwick Manor on St. Crispin's Day, 1887.

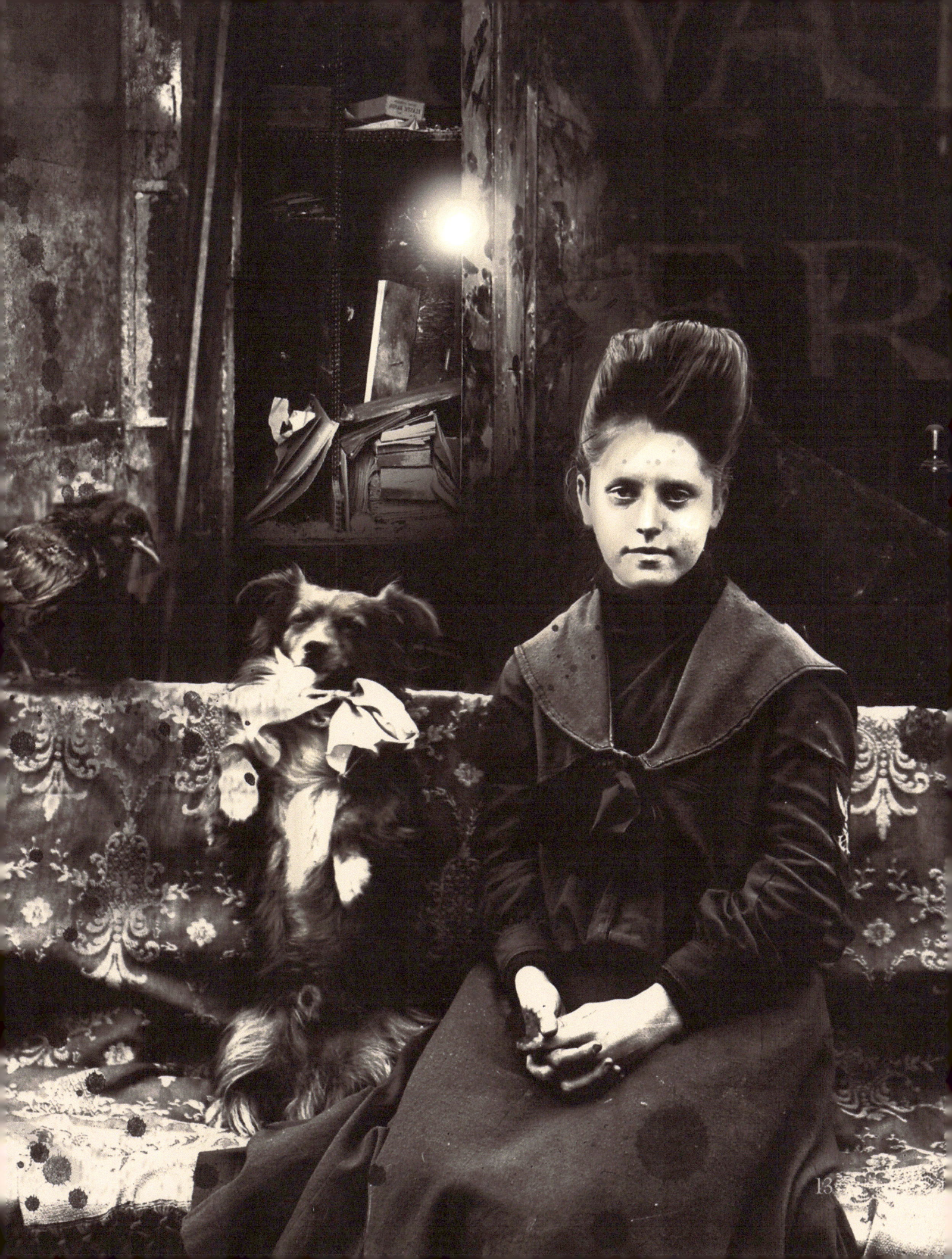

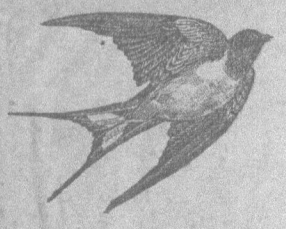

Edwin Countertop McGraw
and his attendant
View A Cathedral

Some days were worse than others. It was on rainy days Edwin felt the effects of gravity most of all, and his above average sized head would list to one side or the other causing him to take on a perplexed appearance to those unaware of his condition. It was for this reason he was forever seen in public with his attendant, Melchior, who, when things got really bad, would walk behind Edwin and hold his head upright until such time as he could get himself home and into a horizontal position.

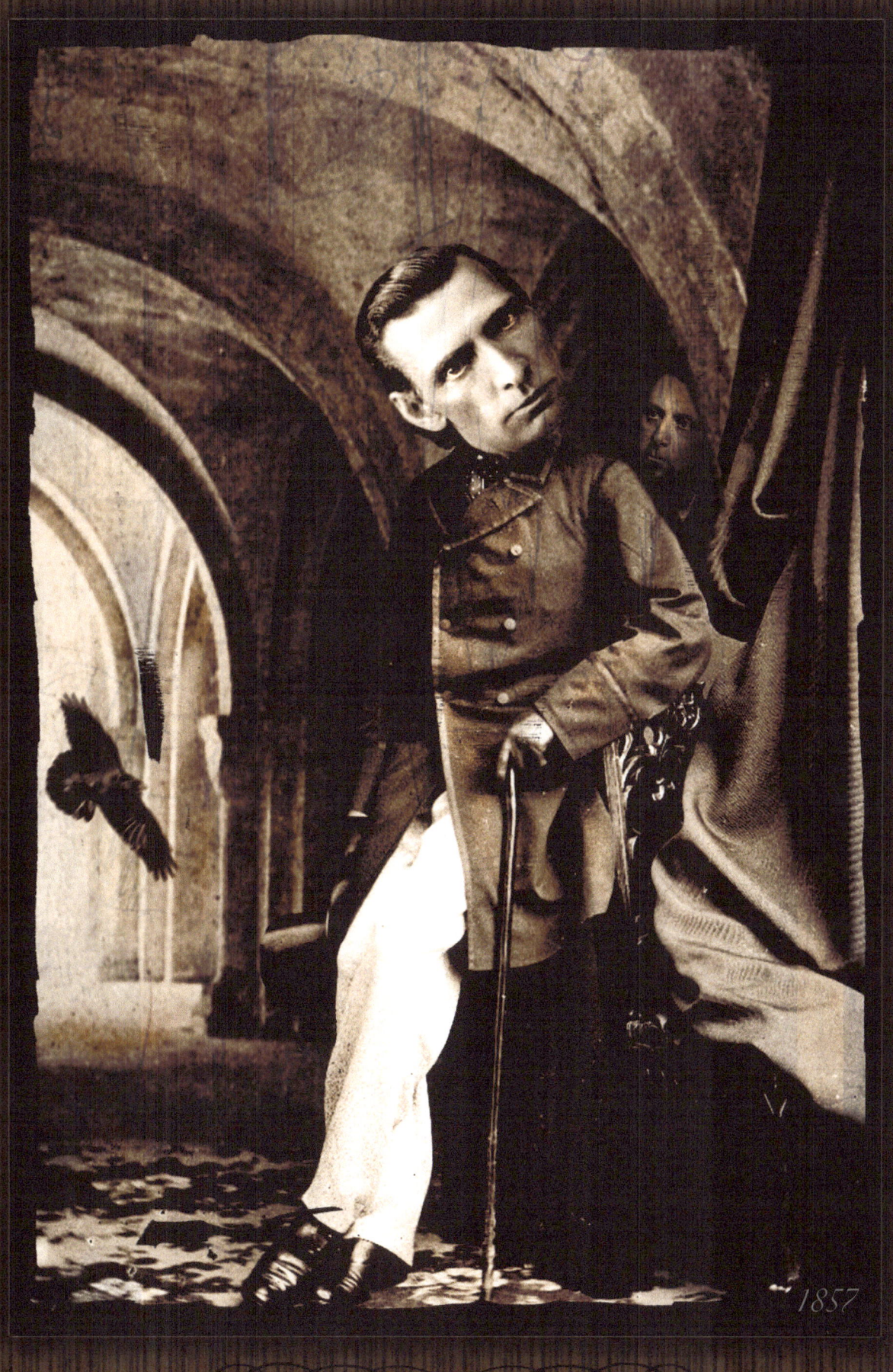

1857

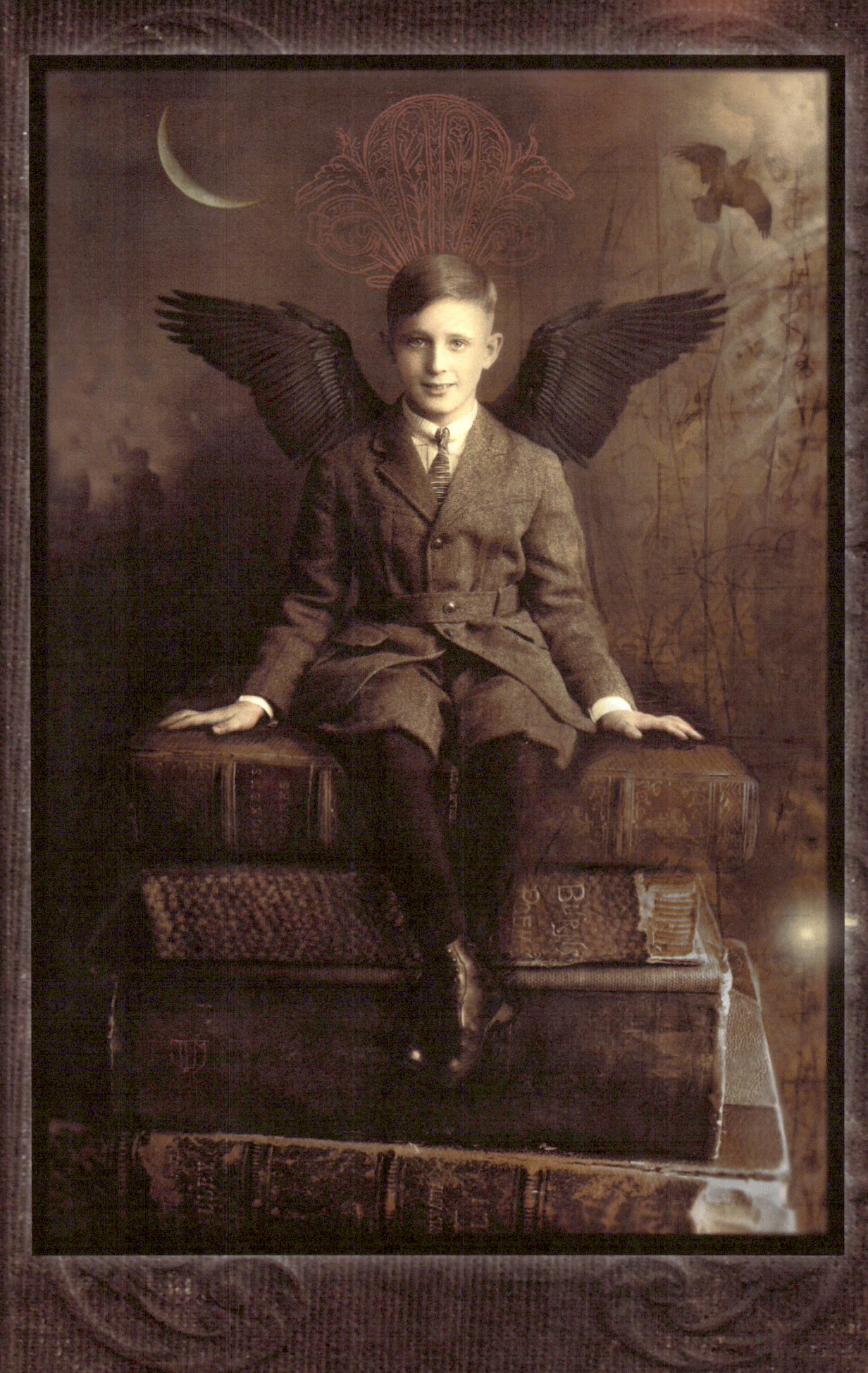

The Guardian

Ever-present boy of light

He sits atop the books by night

To keep them safe from theft or harm

His watch he keeps until the morn

When off he flies to slumber sweet

Tucked in amongst the volumes neat

- H. Vitae

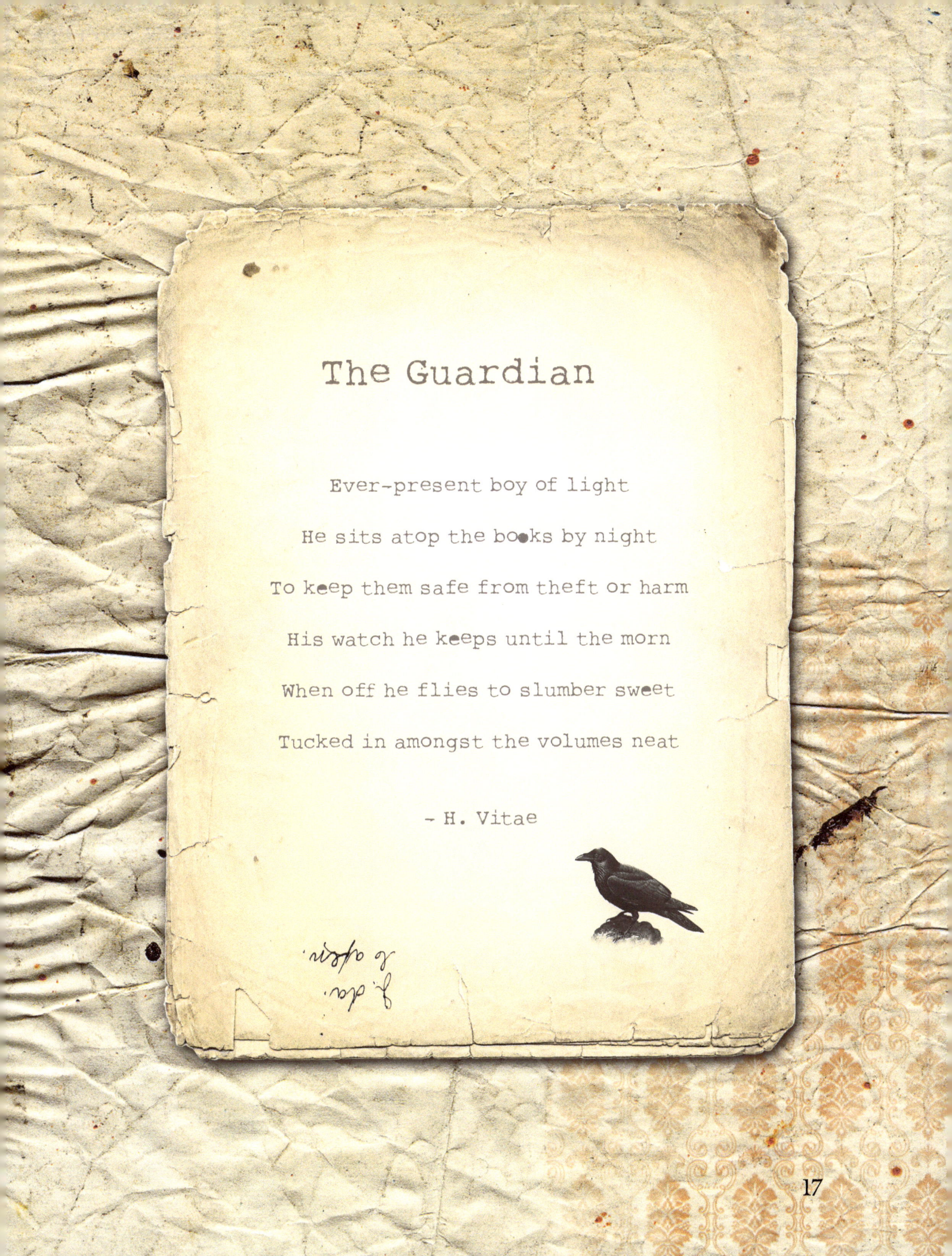

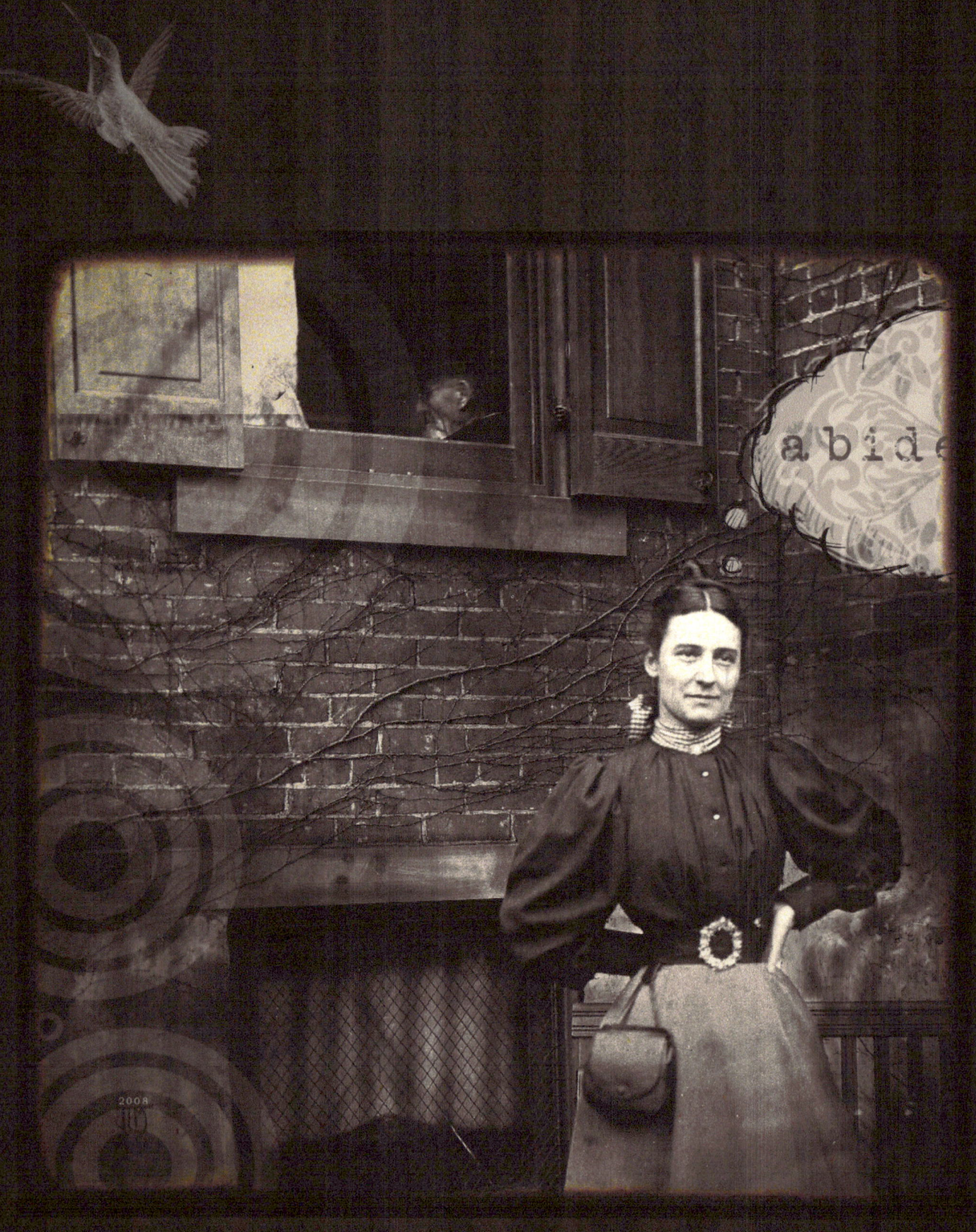

abide

Away I Stray

I had a thousand voices

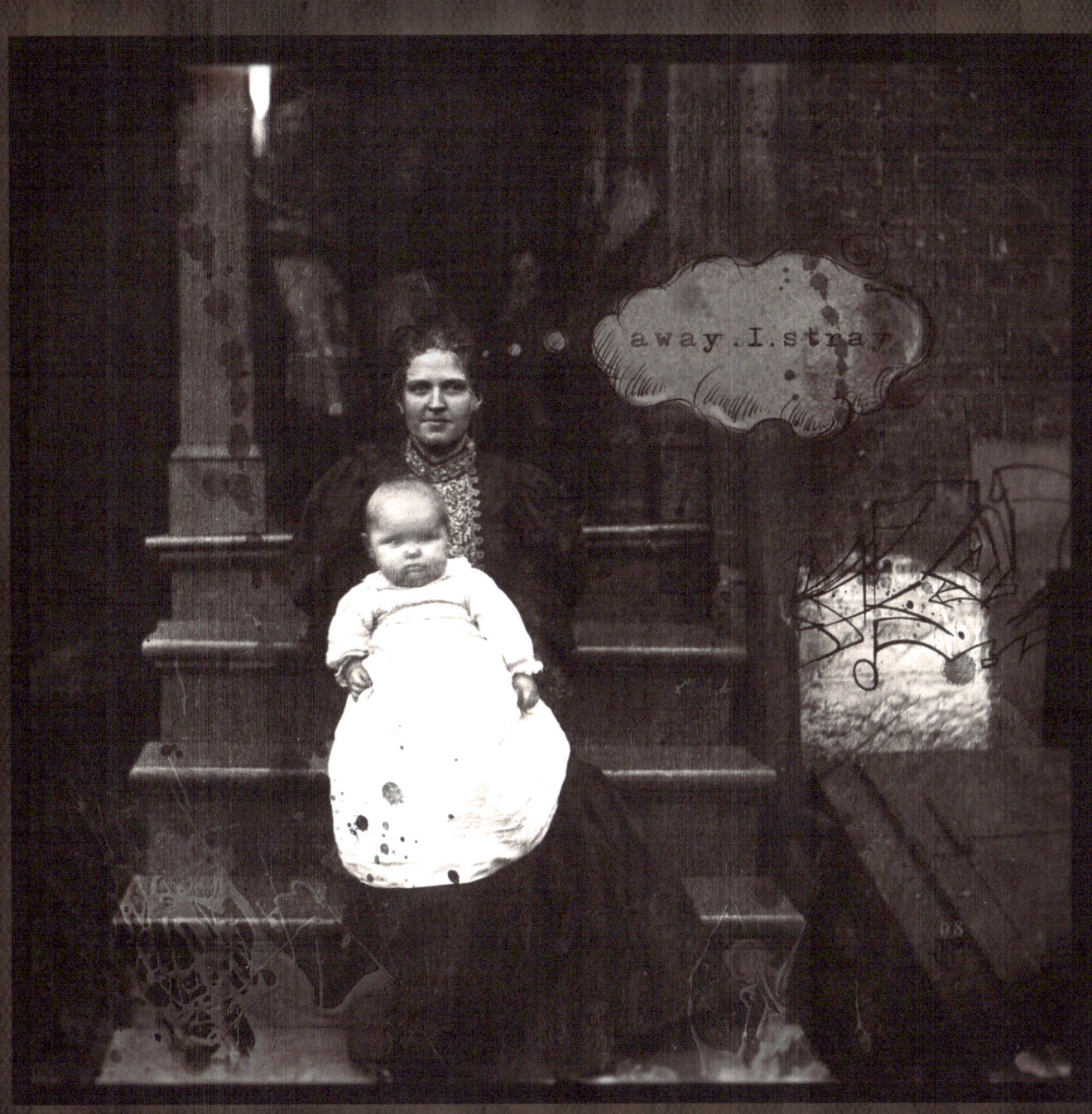

away.I.stray

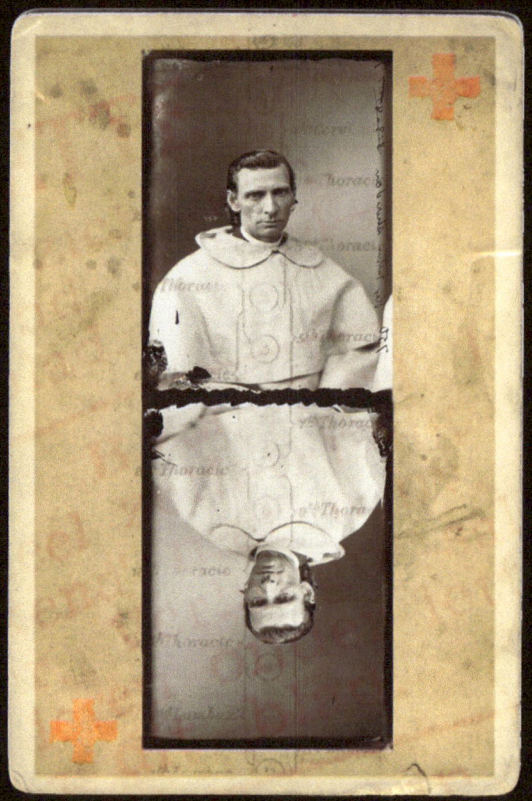

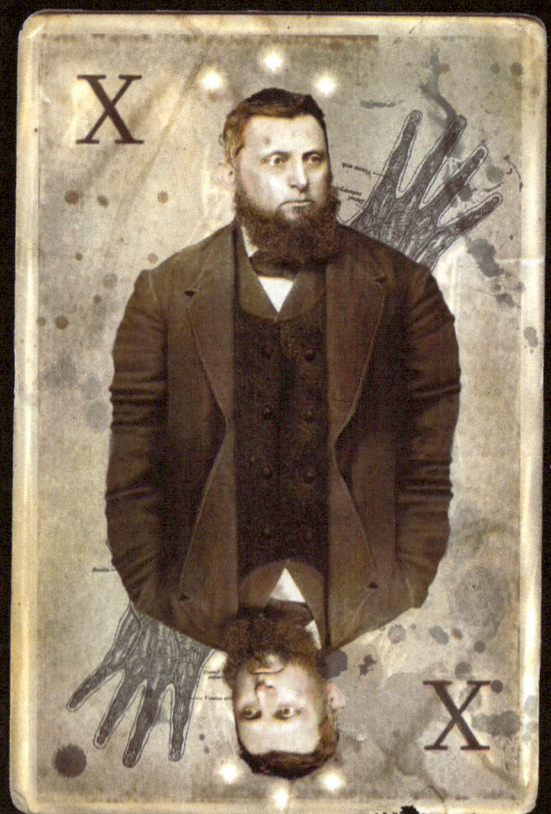

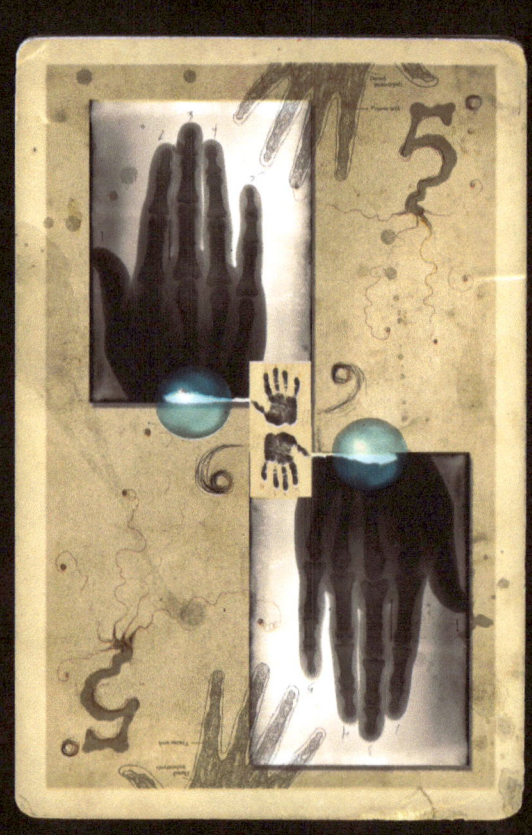

+, X, and 5th degree cards representing remnants of a *Secret Societies* deck.

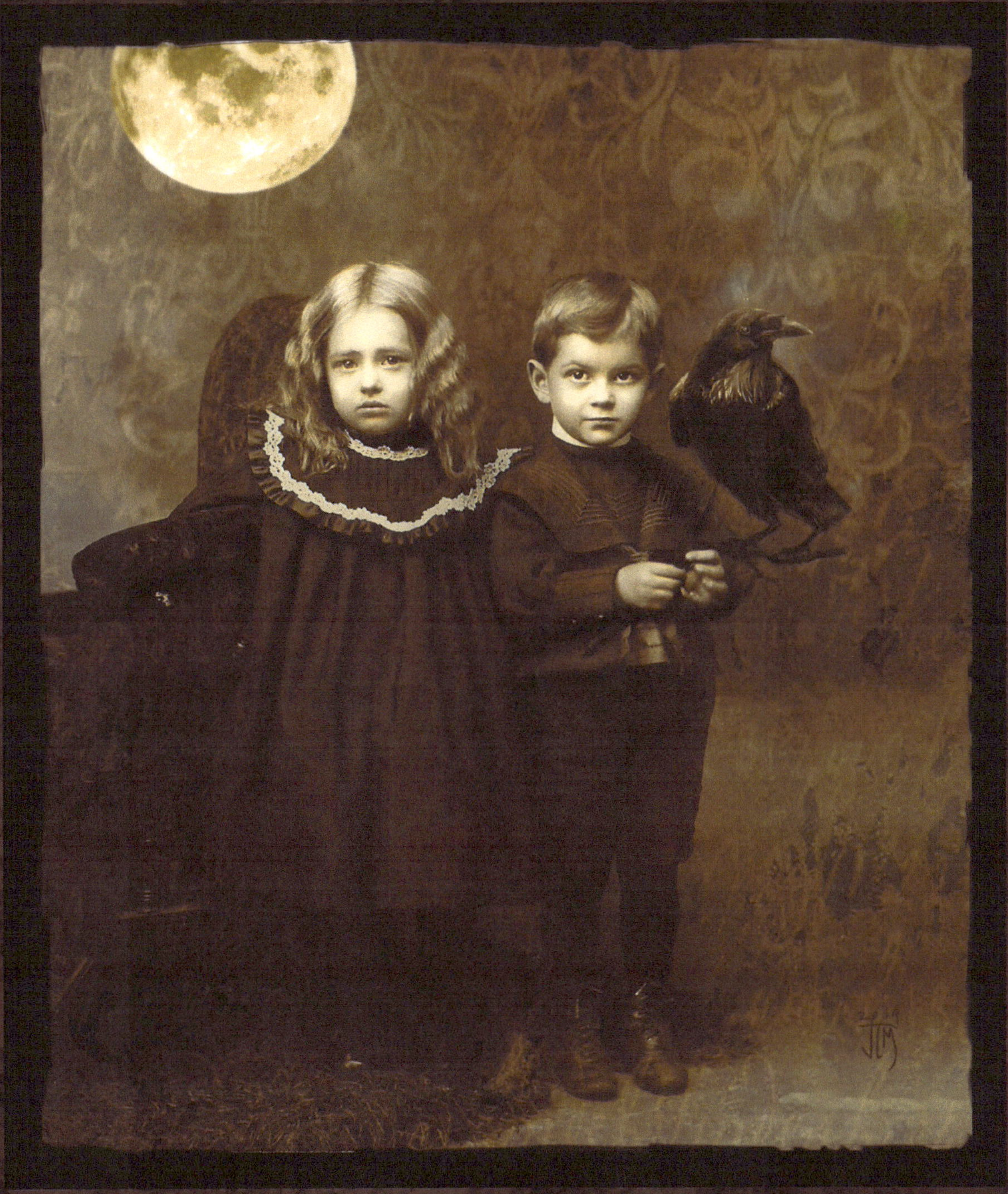

The Blackbough Twins

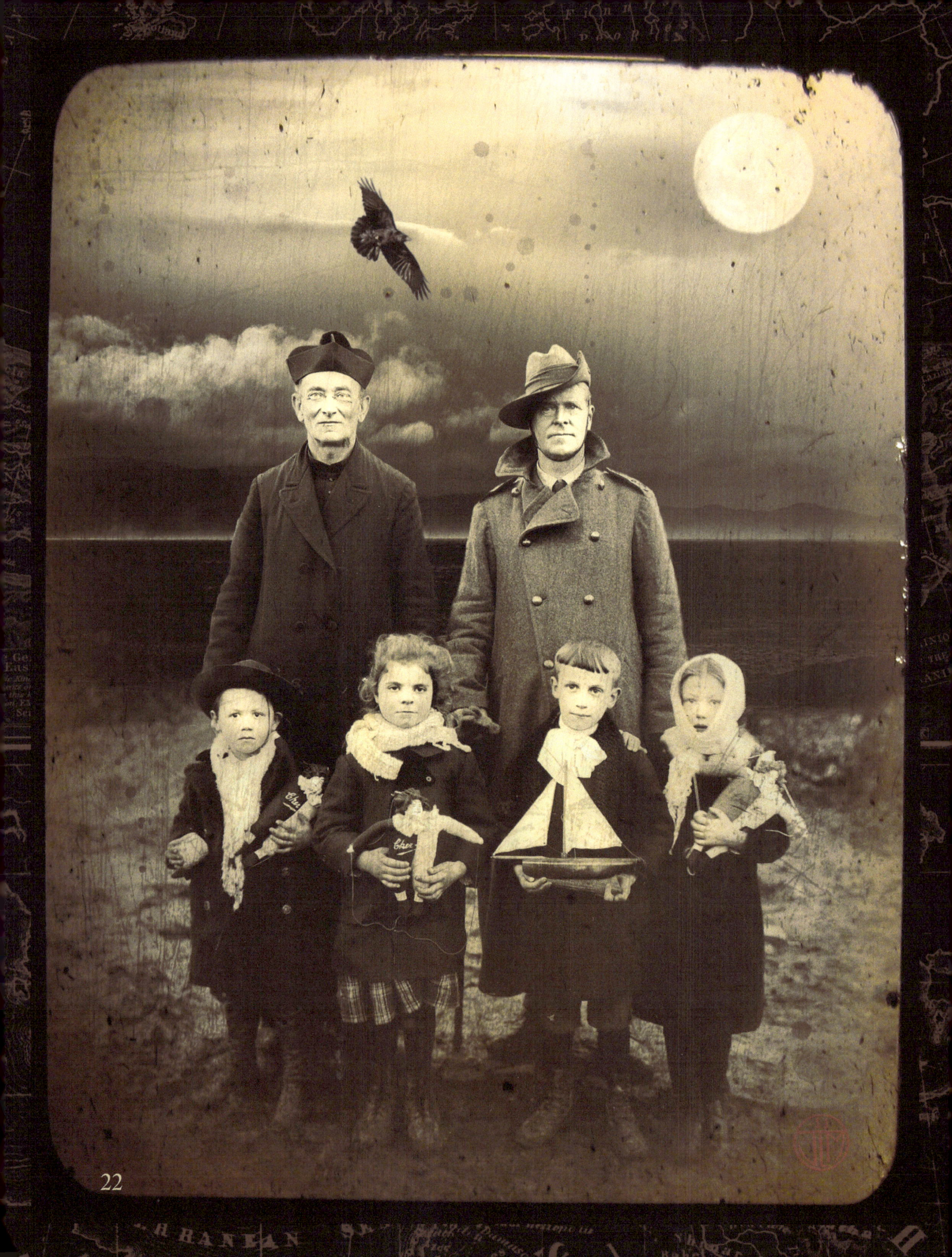

Unlikely Family At The World's End

They were each allowed a single toy on this very last outing. Inexplicably,
three of the four chose their *Cher Ami* dolls, remembering fondly the
story of the famed homing pigeon, which had been trained by American
pigeoneers, who helped save the Lost Battalion of the 77th Division
in the battle of the Argonne, October 1918. Unlike the others, Little
Brandolin hated birds, and any mention of *C. Ami* caused him to break
out in hives. He chose instead his simple yet buoyant model sailboat.
Together with Padre Firebrand and Captain Beaulardon they formed an
unlikely family, who with surprisingly little emotion, watched the final
moonrise.

The Dreadsboro Hats Tragedy

The Dreadsboro sisters purchased their hats on the same day, at the same fair in Gypsypox, from the very same vendor, yet the hats forever refused to acknowledge one another. No matter how the sisters positioned themselves or however quickly they re-positioned themselves, the hats would look in opposite directions. Eventually this aggravated indifference turned to simmering hatred and finally to catastrophic violence. One night Eula and Mania were awoken by agonized shrieks and shuffling sounds. Upon locating the source of the disturbance, naught remained of the hats but scattered black and white feathers and two quiet beaks.

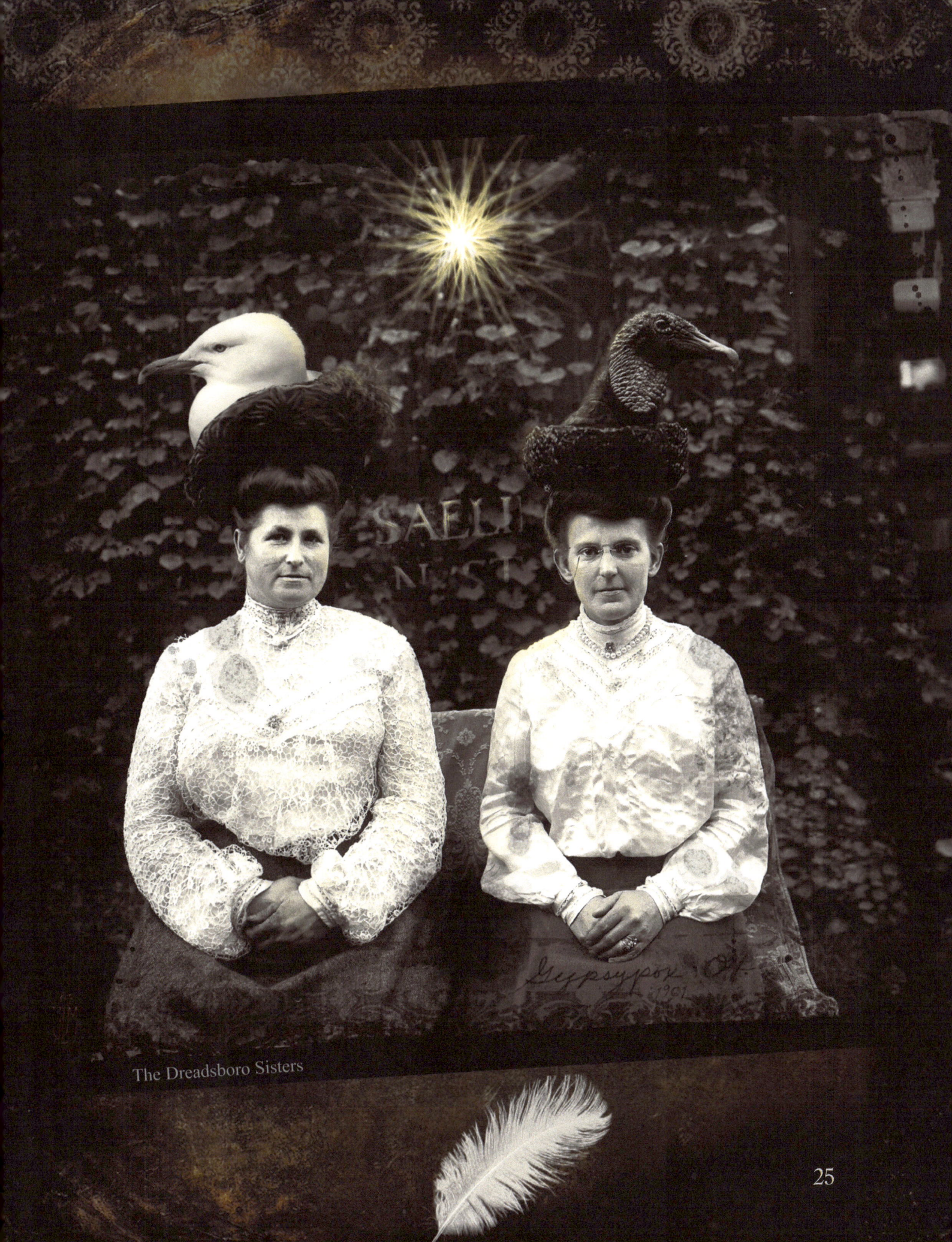

The Dreadsboro Sisters

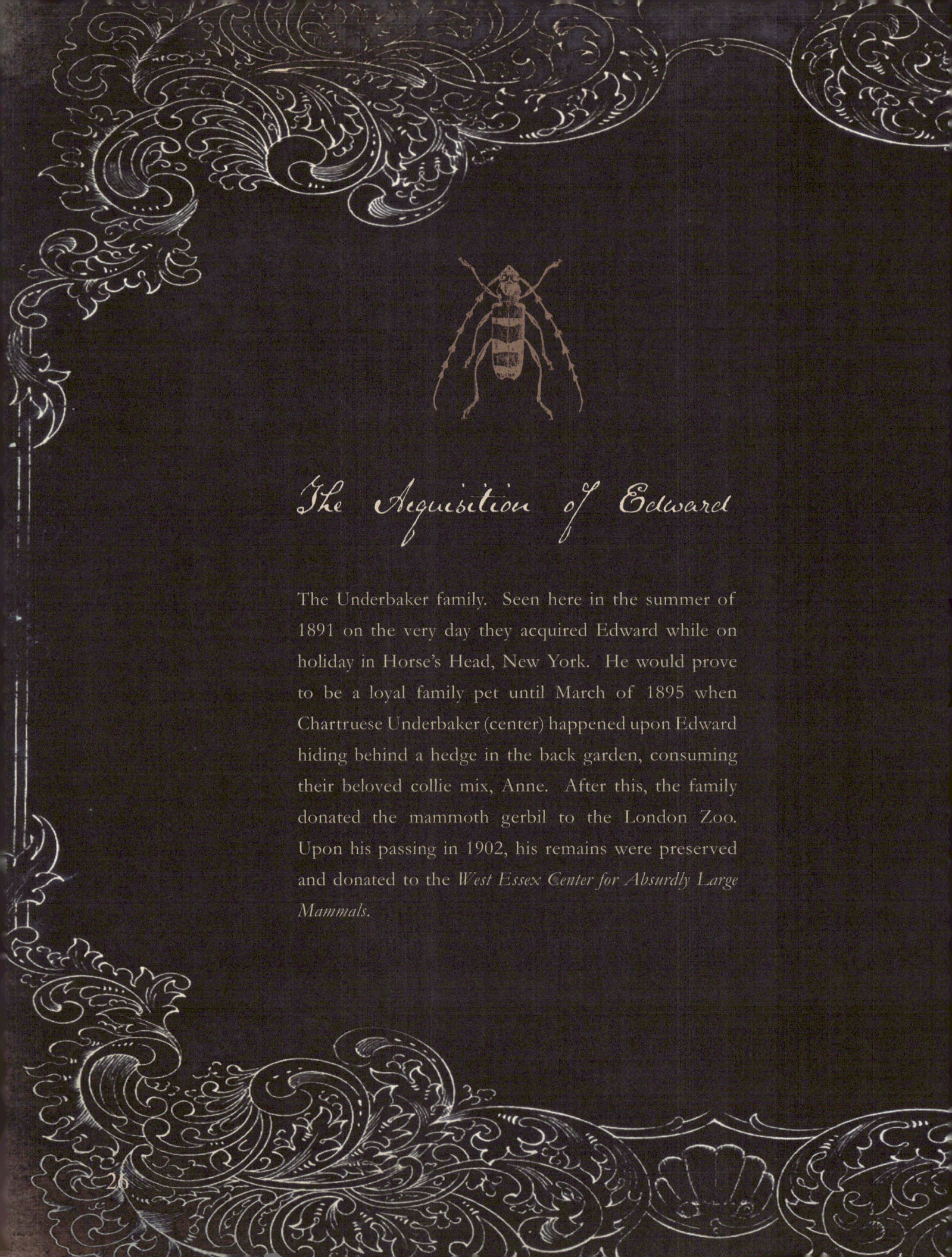

The Acquisition of Edward

The Underbaker family. Seen here in the summer of 1891 on the very day they acquired Edward while on holiday in Horse's Head, New York. He would prove to be a loyal family pet until March of 1895 when Chartruese Underbaker (center) happened upon Edward hiding behind a hedge in the back garden, consuming their beloved collie mix, Anne. After this, the family donated the mammoth gerbil to the London Zoo. Upon his passing in 1902, his remains were preserved and donated to the *West Essex Center for Absurdly Large Mammals.*

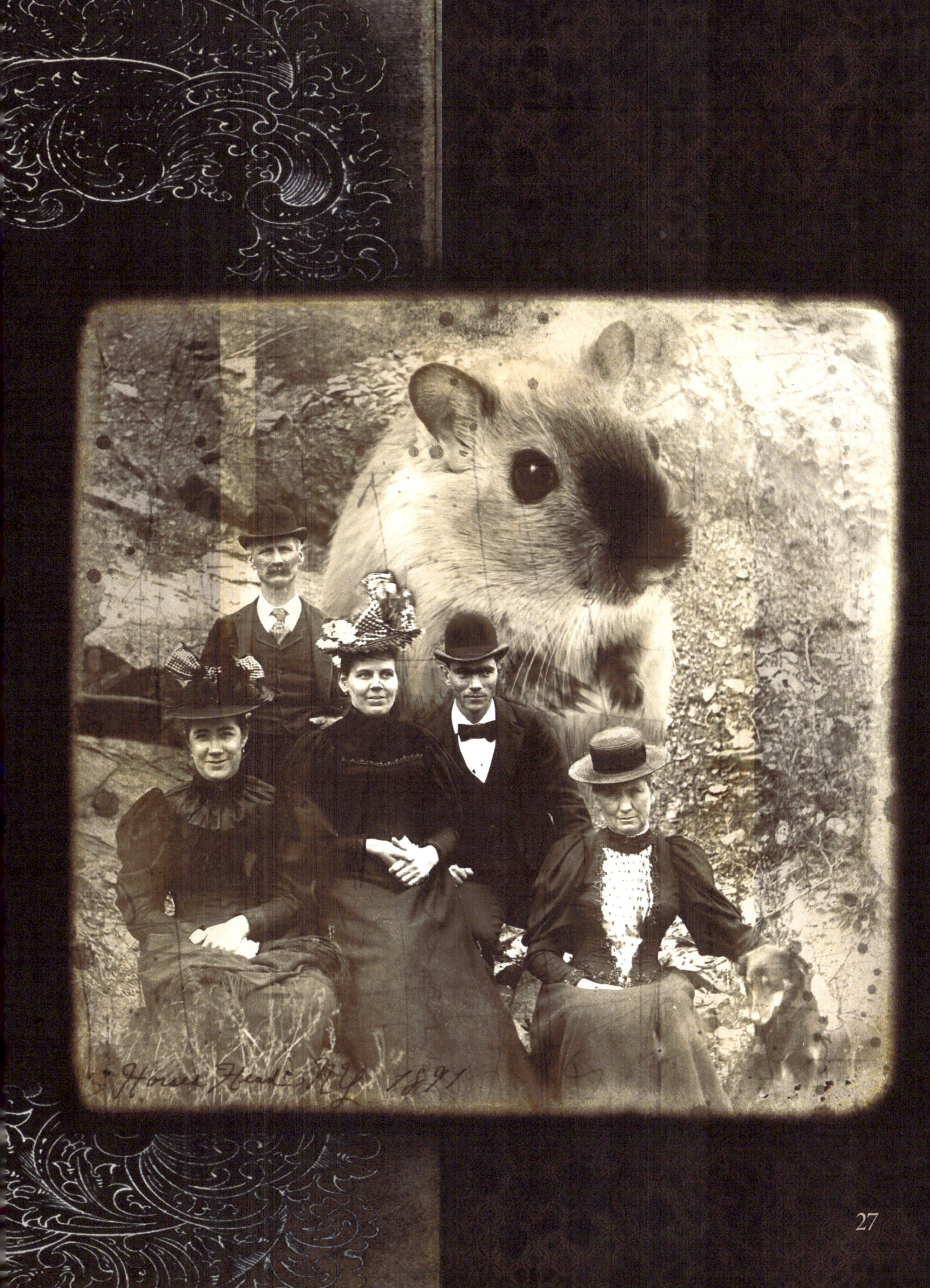

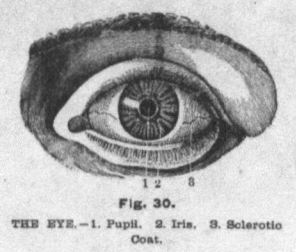

Fig. 30.

THE EYE.—1. Pupil. 2. Iris. 3. Sclerotic
Coat.

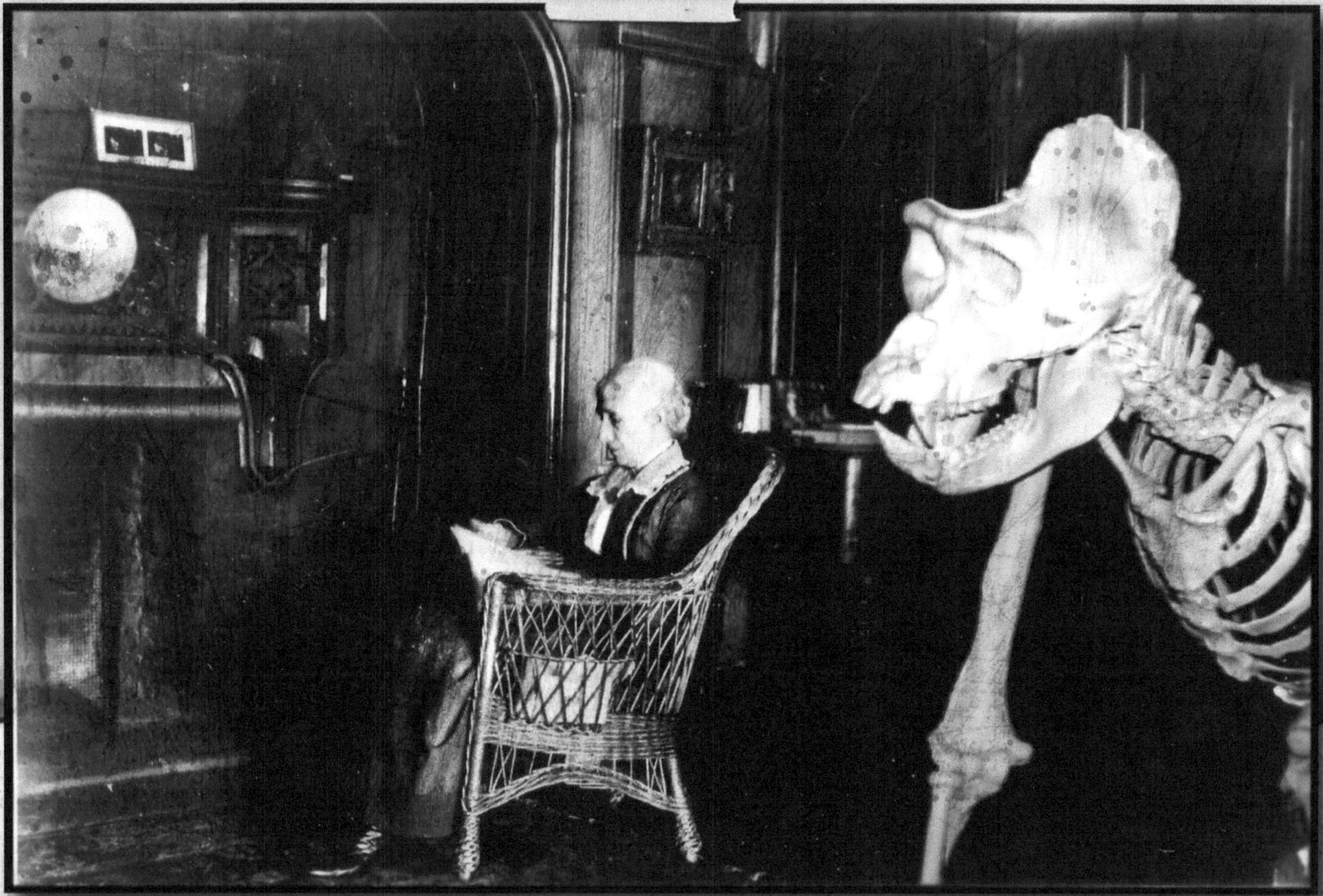

Elspith Unaware

Elspith noticed neither the tiny moon that had found its way into her sitting room via the fireplace nor the creature lurking just behind her back as she sat absorbed in a book. The creature, on the other hand, was fully aware.

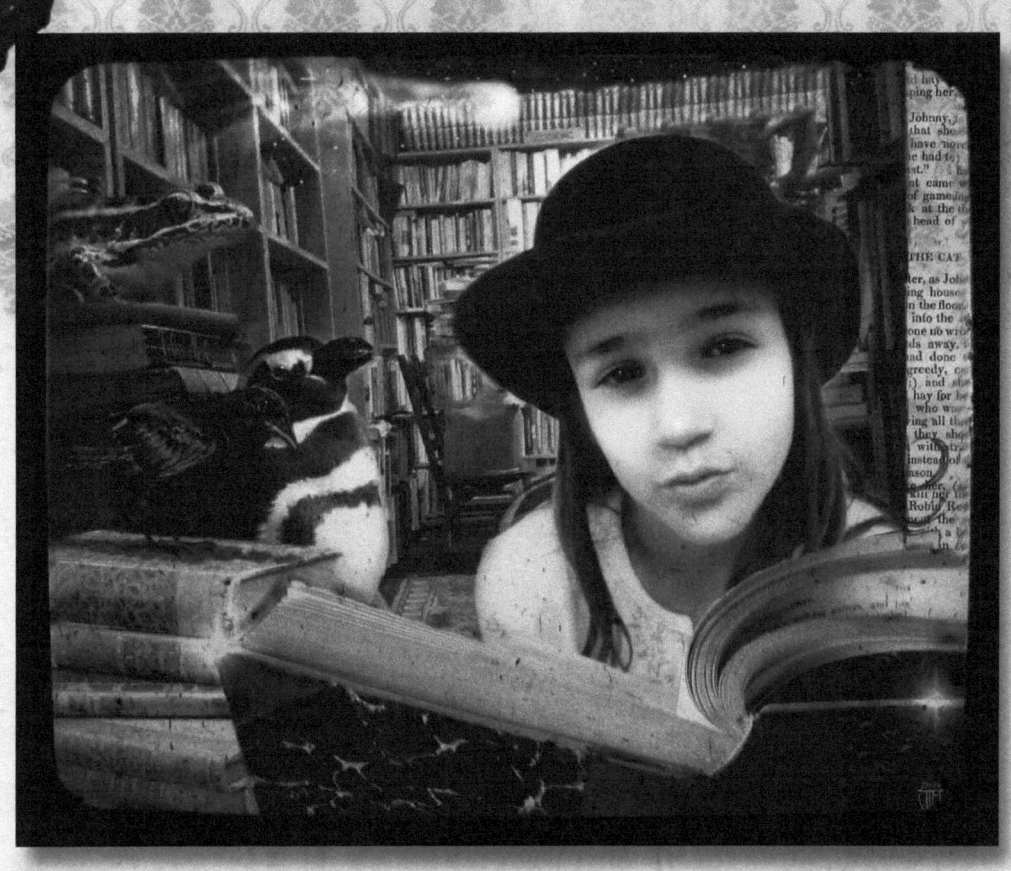

Faithful Friends, Listen

"In the vast library of the universe, the Book of
Starlight was opened by a child who wanted nothing
more than to read to the birds. Though the myths
would change with each telling, they would never
fade away. The Book would not be silent. The child,
Avery, was just one chapter. The birds were the
words. Each individual life was a paragraph."

~Michael Titus, "The Girl Who Read To Birds"

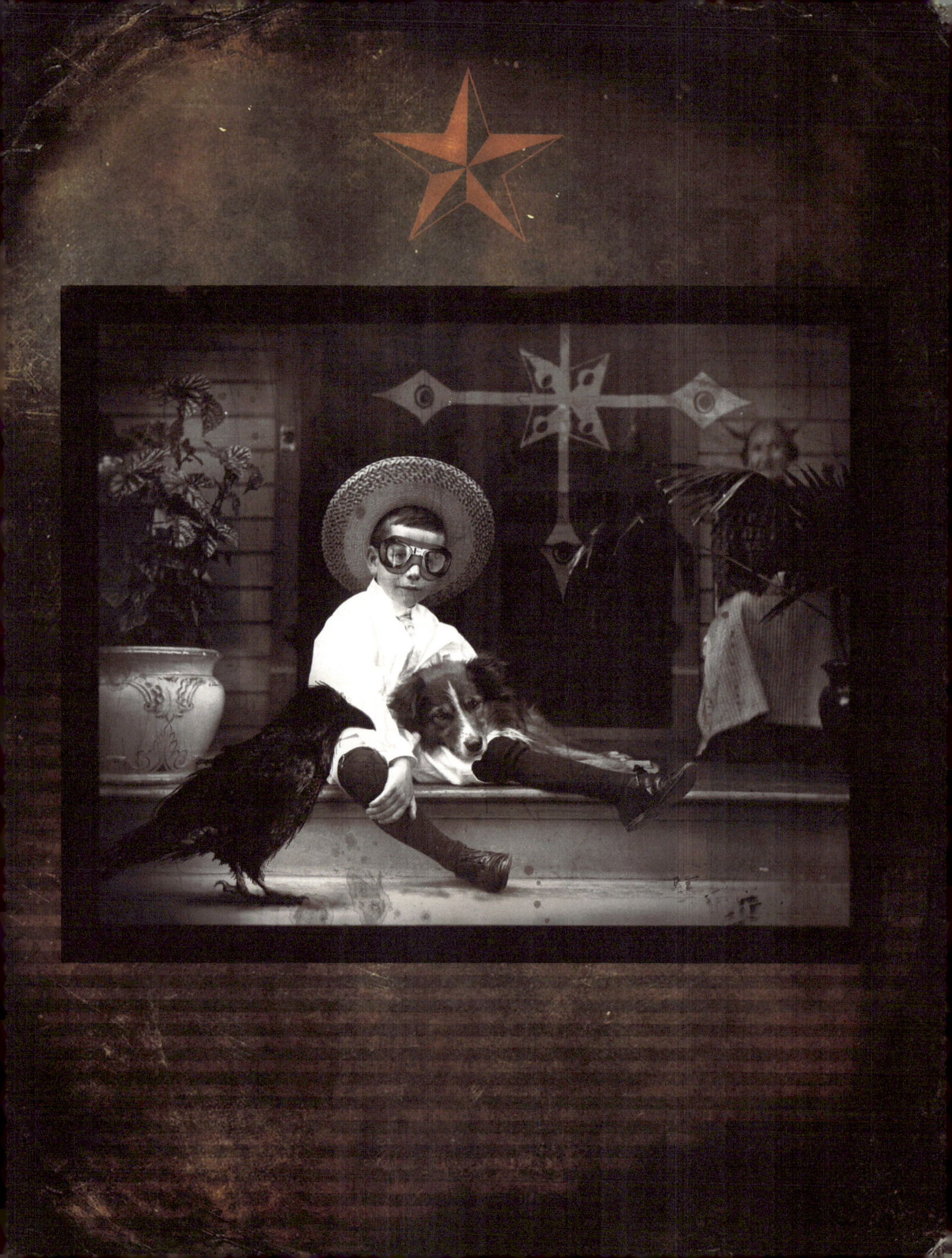

Summoning The Great
Continuum

They met on Gran's front porch each June 12th to summon the powers of *The Great Continuum*. There was little Bartie with his fashionable science goggles, Pathos, the slumberhound, forever at Bartie's side, and Chlorimonia, the raven who was considered large for a bird of her type but still within normal limits. Gran Mizrabelle who sat watch over the band of friends opted out of the proceedings each year, excusing herself with '*another bout of the jitters.*' This is the only known photograph of the event.

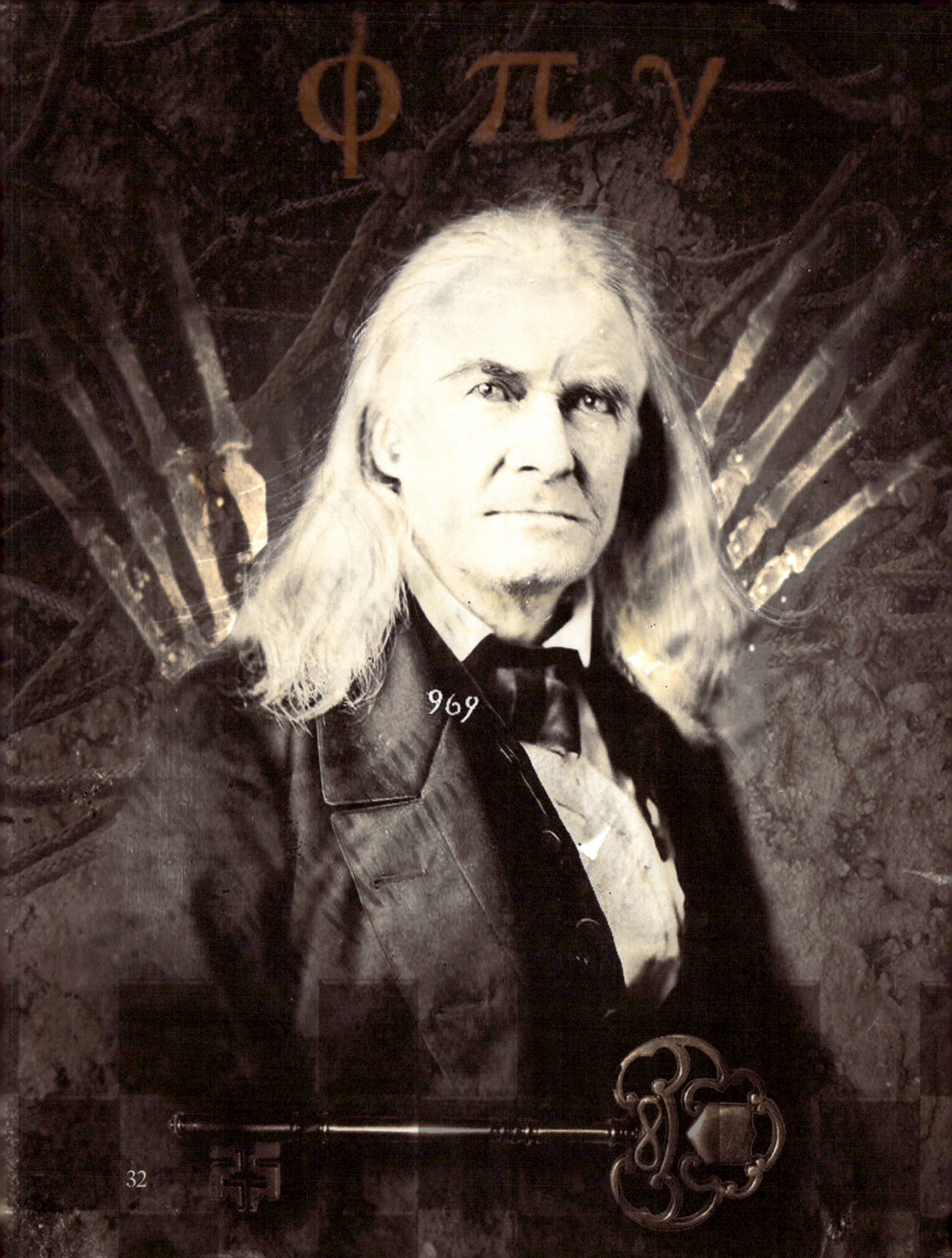

ΦΠΥ

969

hans leftie agrippa

Hans Agrippa was known to his closest friends as Leftie due to the fact that he was prone to spasms of the left side of his body when stressed or provoked in any way. The West Grumbly Bureau of Obscure Dance studied his one-sided movements and entered the subsequent dance quintet created from them, entitled "Go Left Young Man," into the *Anatomical Anomaly Dance-Off of 1874* where it received an honorable mention. The '969' seen etched into the photograph of Agrippa was thought to have been a cataloging number, but recent scholarship suggests it may well have been his age at the time of his death, as his signature appears on the death certificate of mathematician-physician-philosopher Thabit ibn Qurrah of Baghdad in 901 A.D. as well as the Old English Annals of Celestial Observations of 1114 A.D.

Note: As some of you may have observed, this is actually a photo from the Library of Congress Prints & Photographs Division of Edmund Ruffin, the man who is often credited with firing the first shot of the American Civil War.

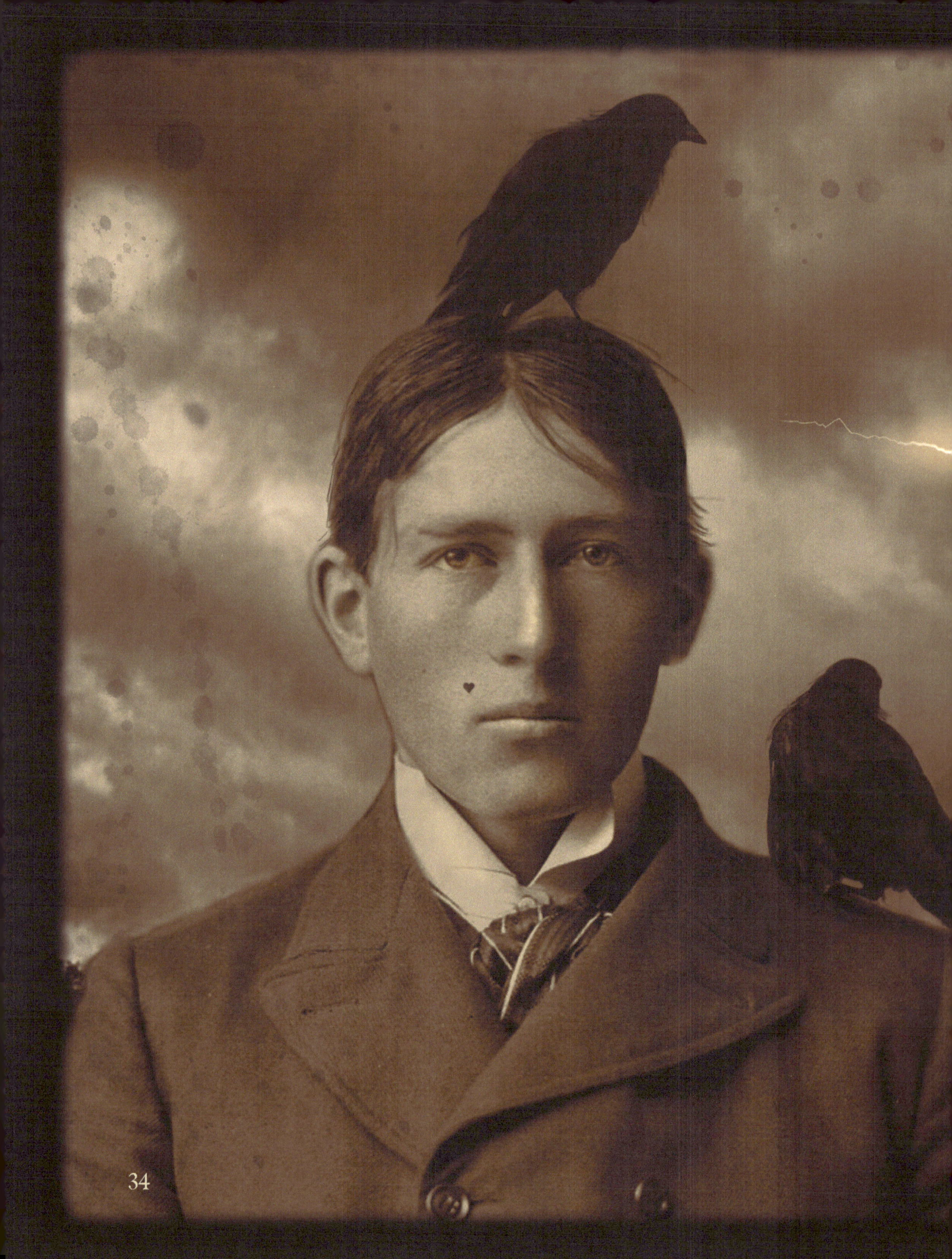

34

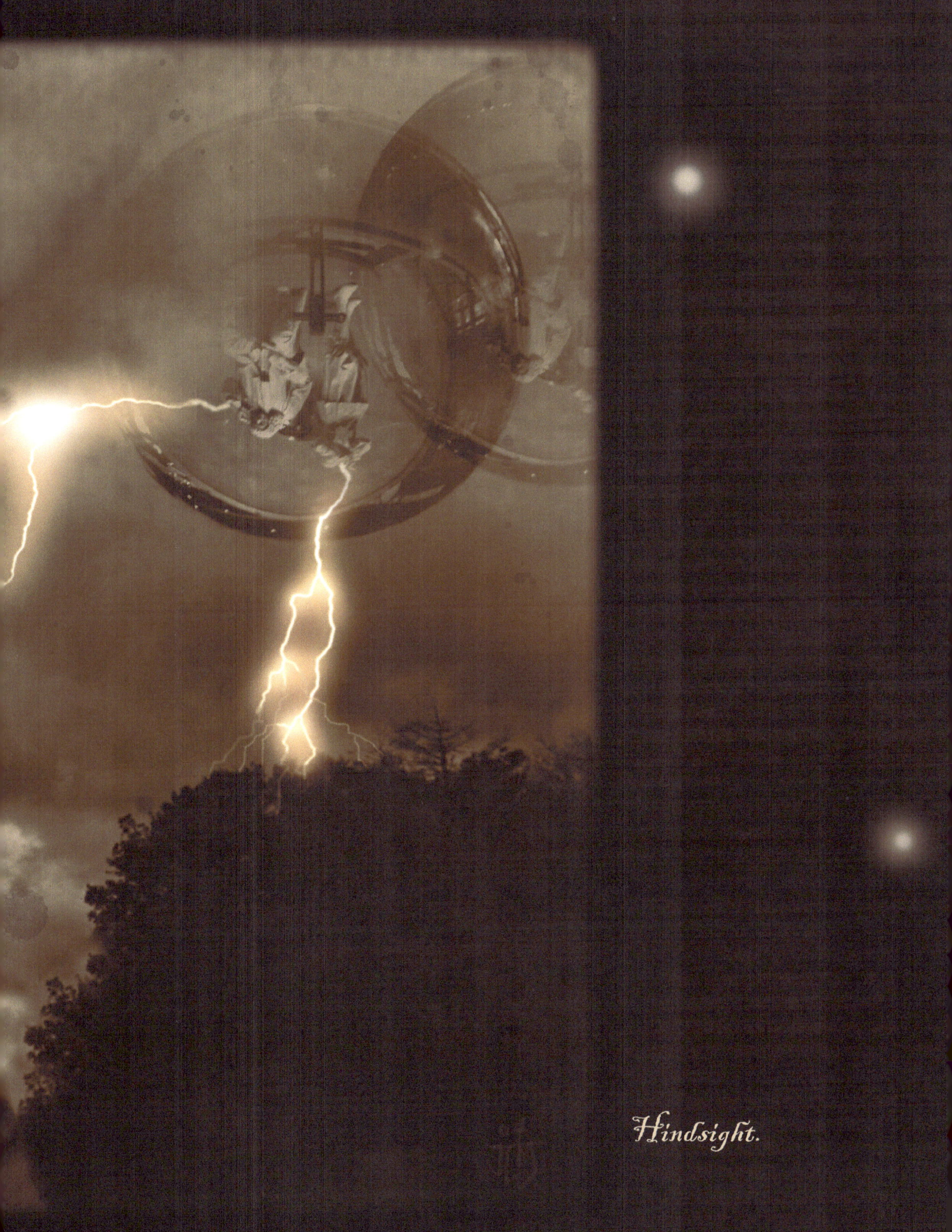

Hindsight.

H.V. Avec

Des Lunettes

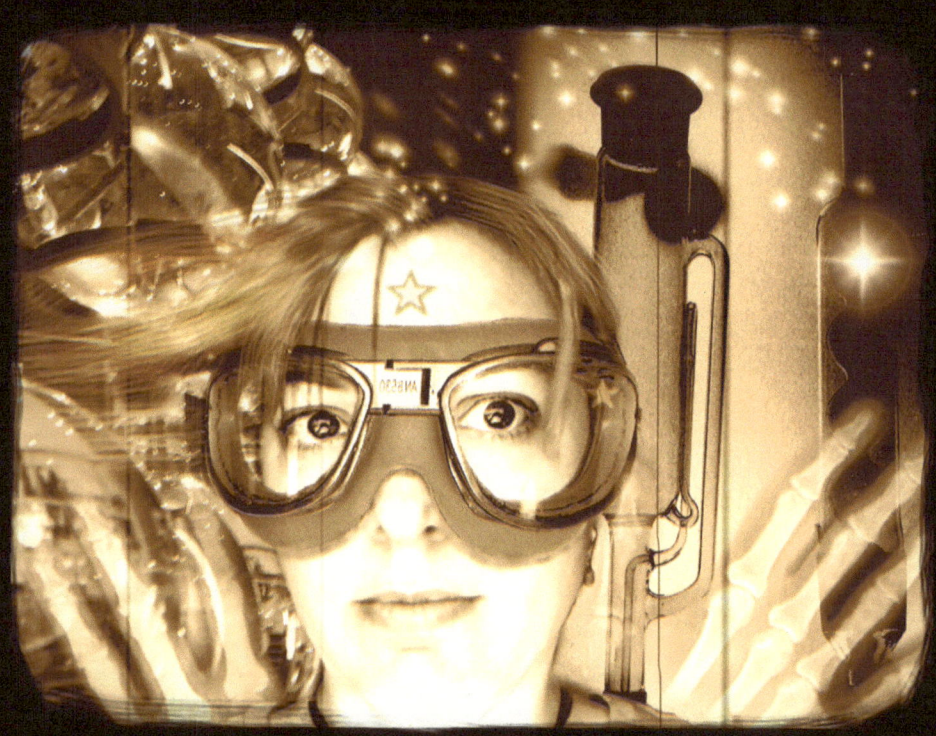

de la Science

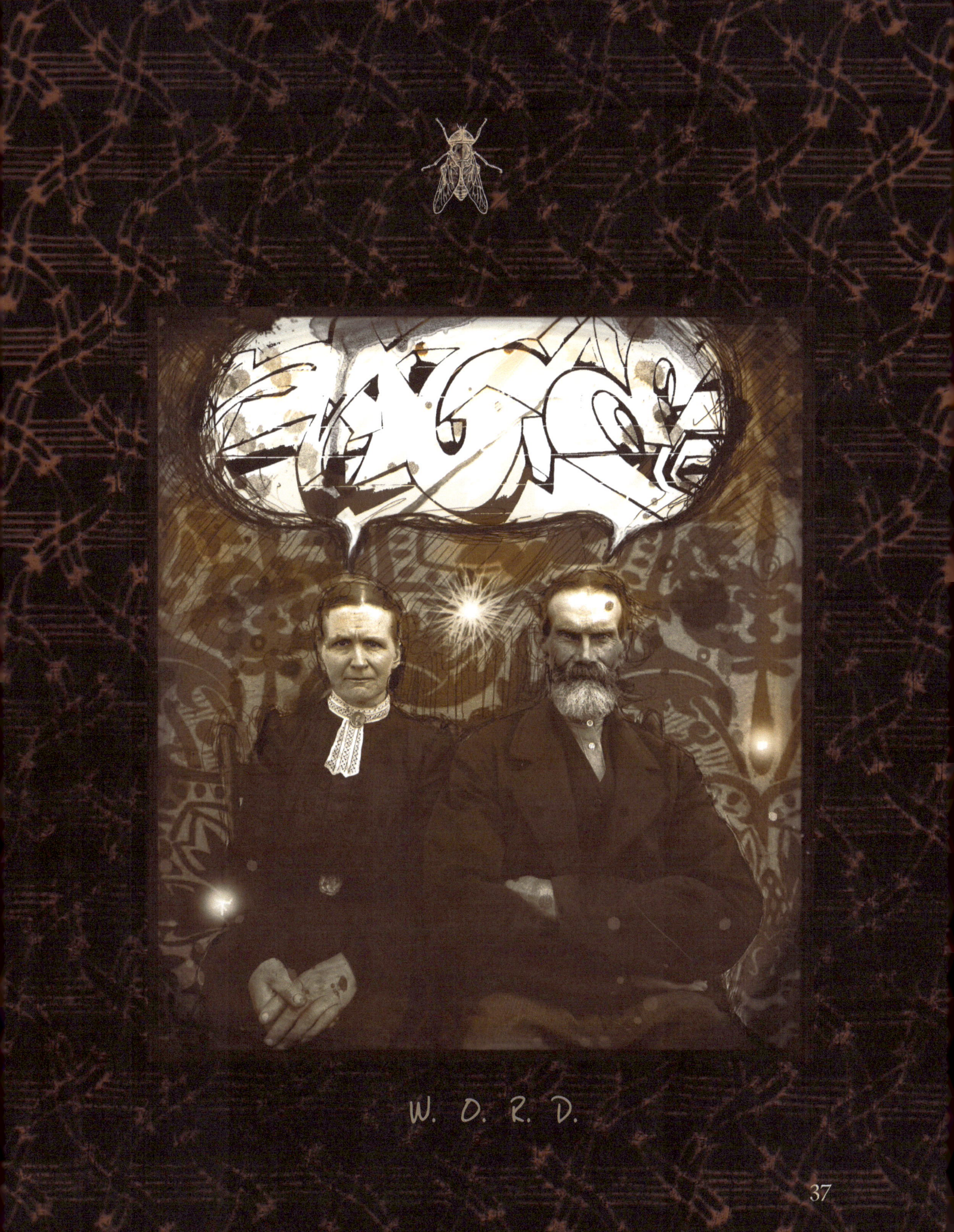

W. O. R. D.

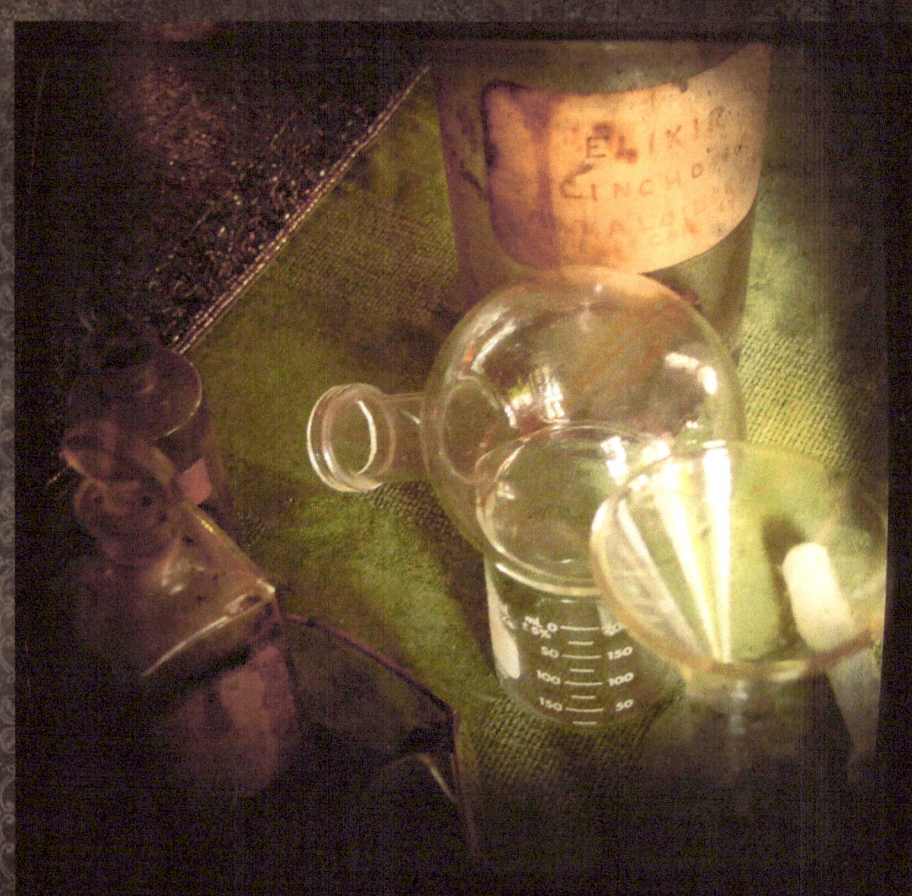

Chemistry.

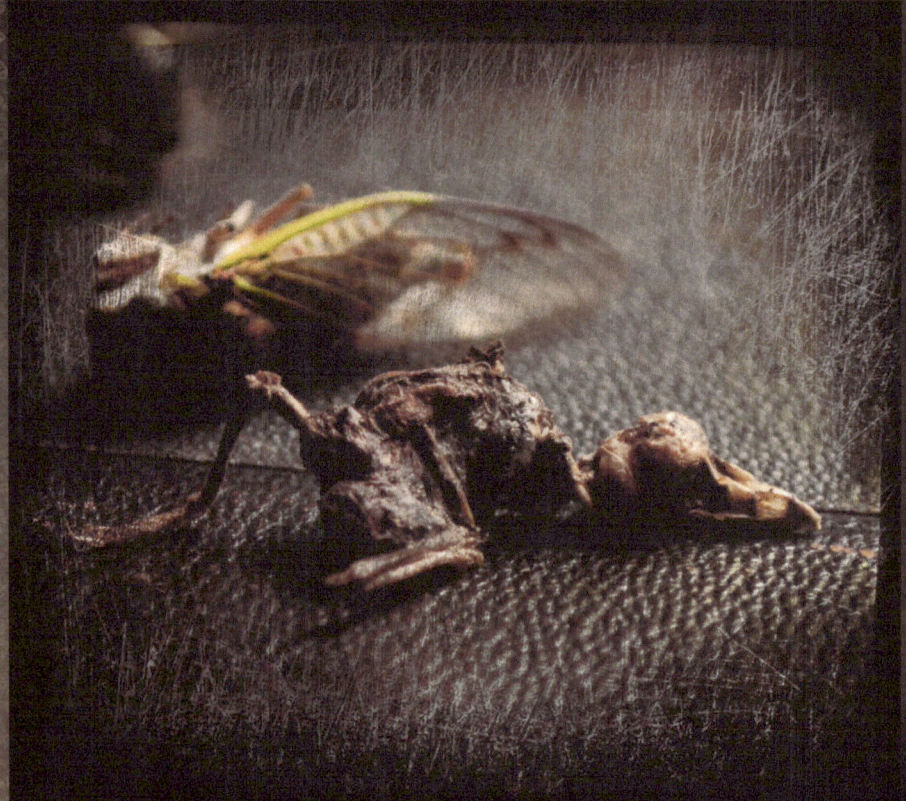

Ex-baby bird and cicada.

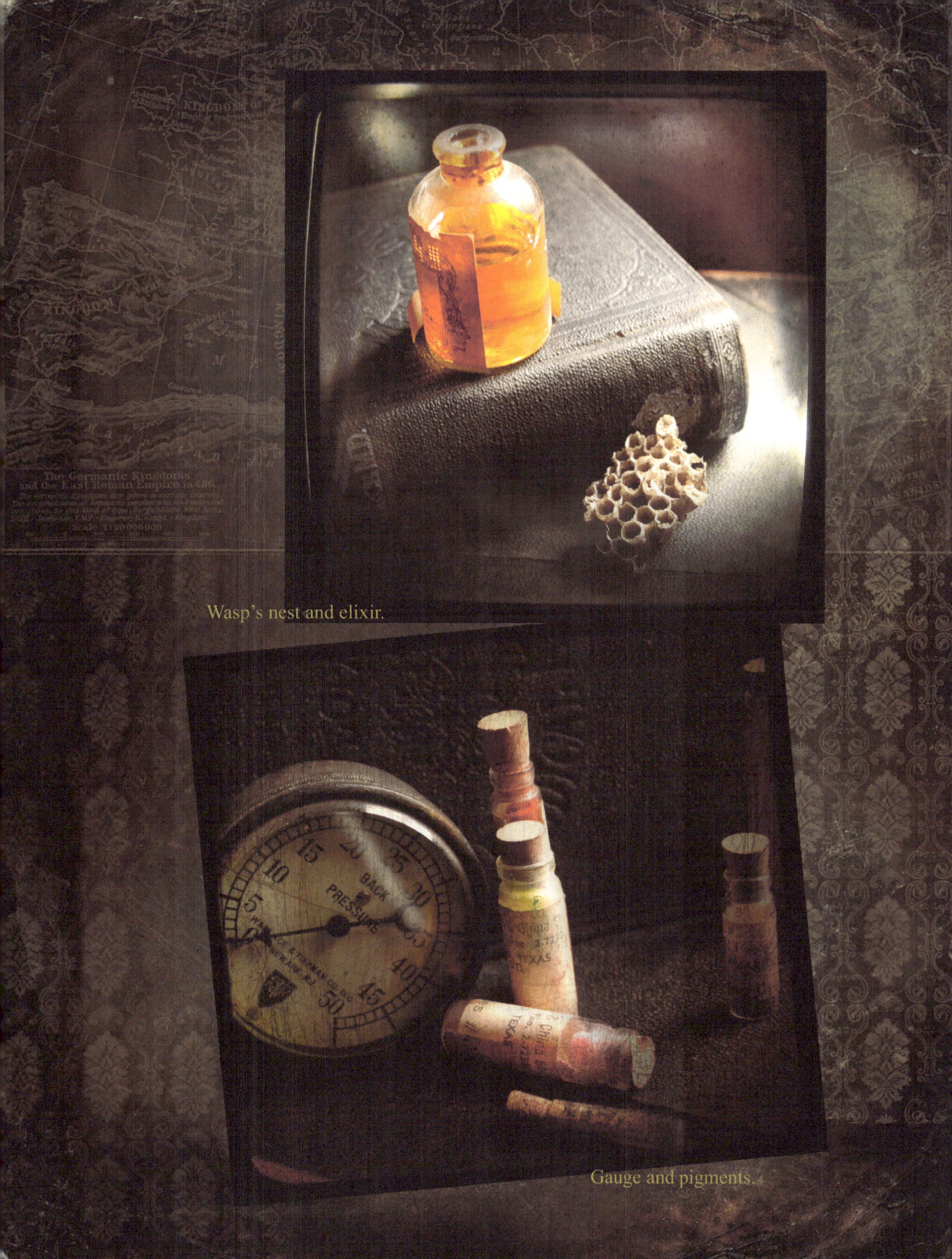

Wasp's nest and elixir.

Gauge and pigments.

IN LOWLY REVERENCE ADORE

No one can clearly remember the day that Augustus
brought home Aunt Fanny as Father came to call her,
though I do recall that it was in the summer. Gus would
keep her on the porch on the whole, although if she was
in the house when we took tea, she would always ask
if it was *'Daaahjeeling,'* sometimes incessantly. She said
little, only three or four sentences and always insensible.
One night she woke up the entire household asking
repeatedly for *'Finsbury.'*

Eventually Mother made Father get rid of her after Gus
chewed on her nose.

We all missed the old girl...

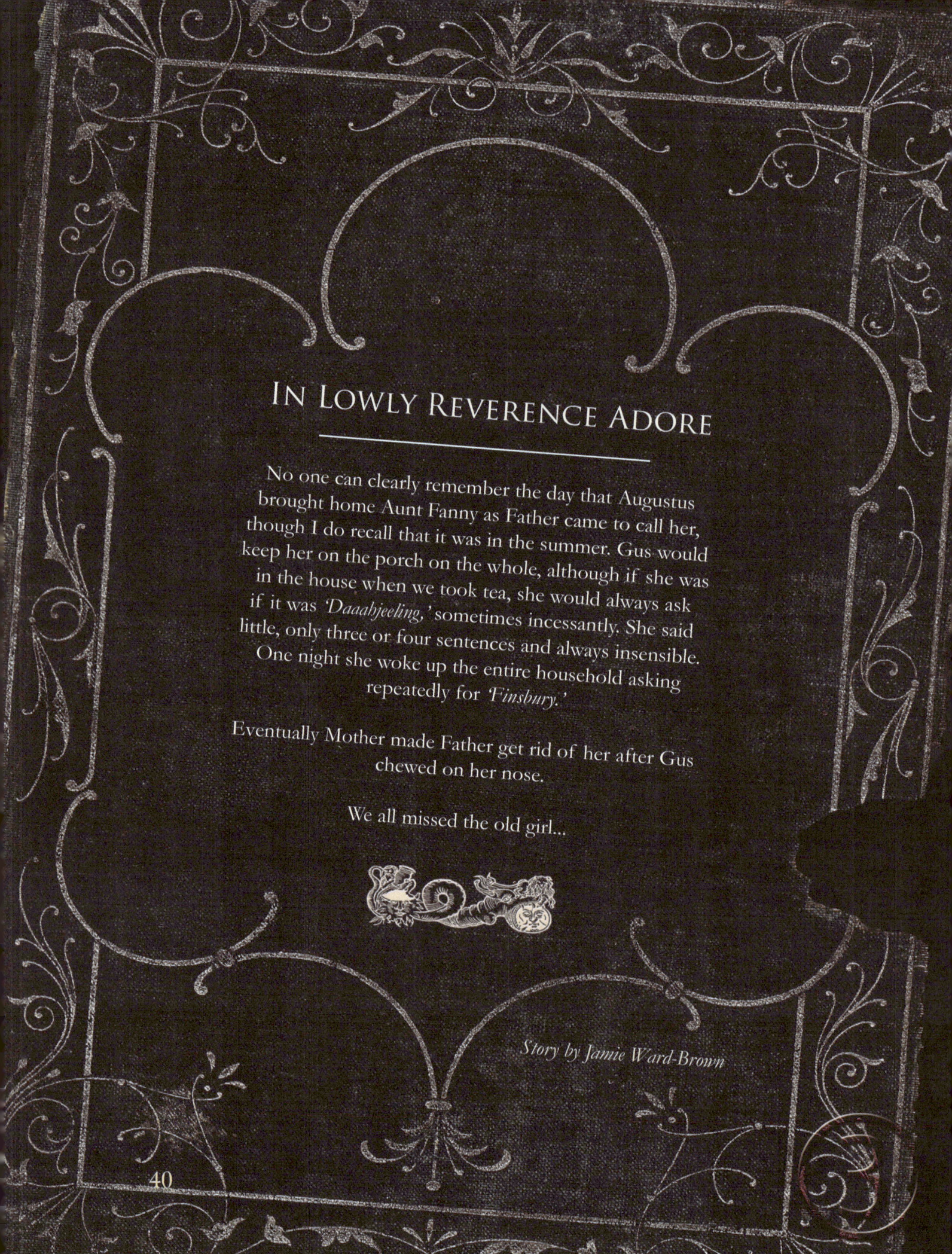

Story by Jamie Ward-Brown

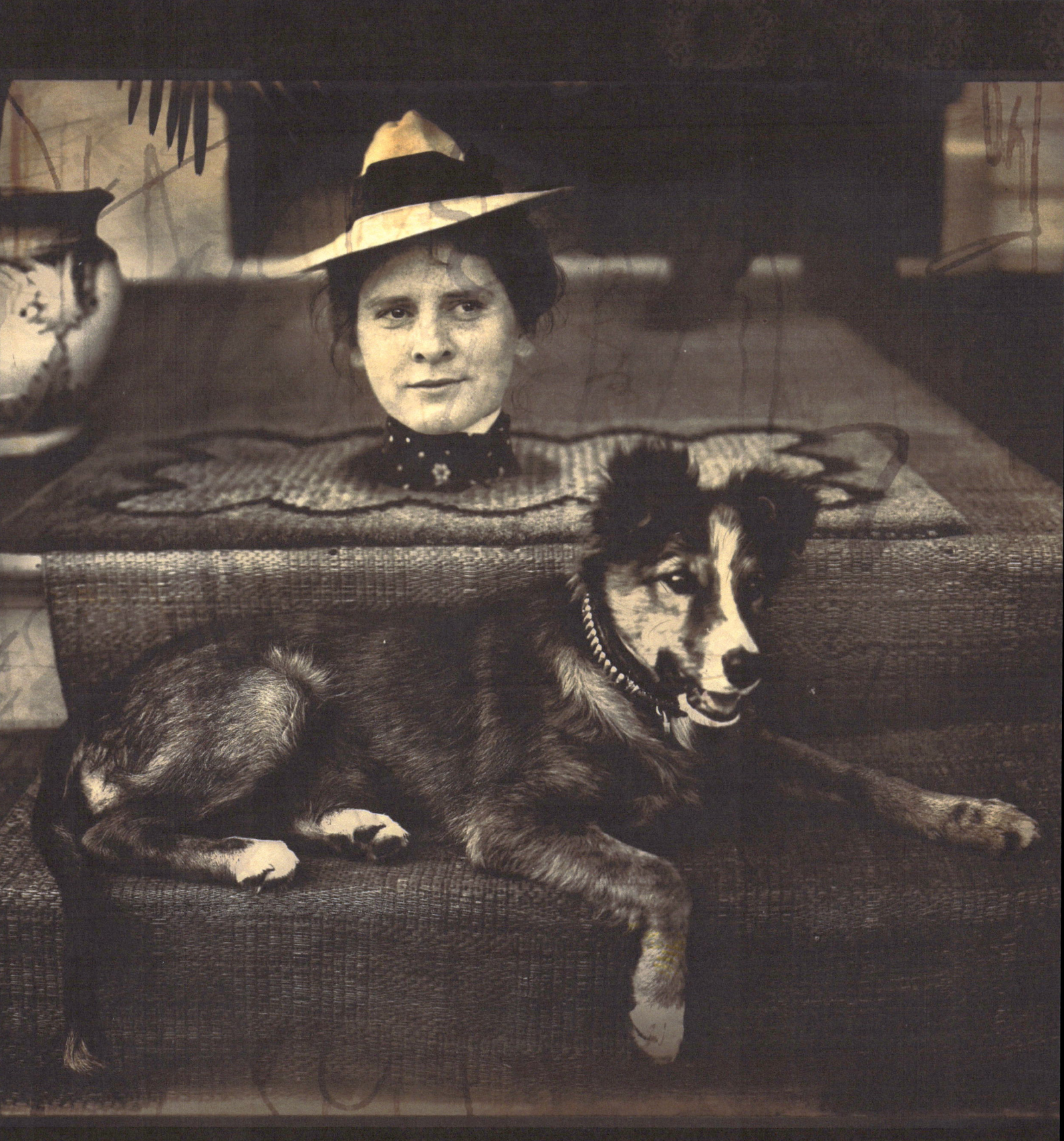

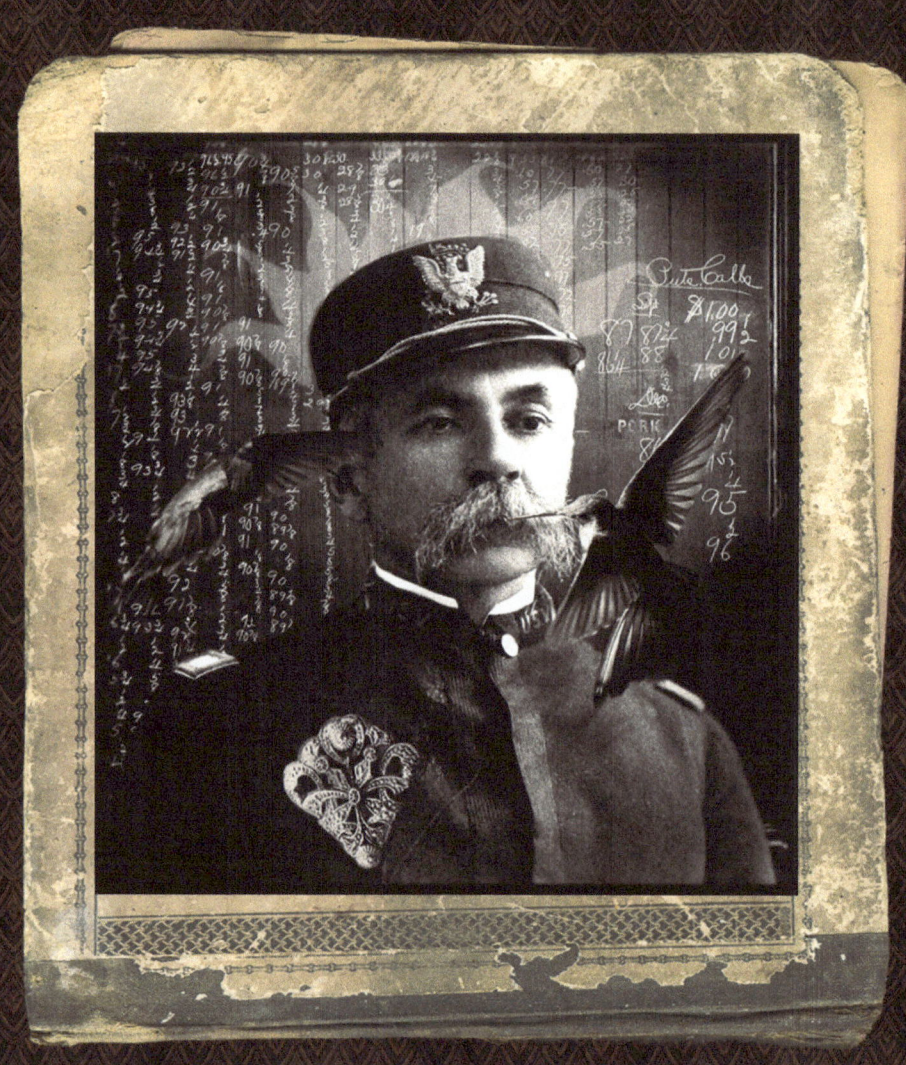

Symbiosis

Without fail, whenever he held completely still they would appear. Buzzing silently around him, slipping their delicate beaks into his mouth, ears, nose, and a few times trying for an eye with no success. Still he did not move. Not a twitch, a blink, a wince. Never did he slap at them, shoo them, or shake his head vigorously in annoyance. From them he received fleeting but intense bursts of camaraderie; from him, they took the sweet nectar of humanity, *aqua vitae*.

And so it goes.

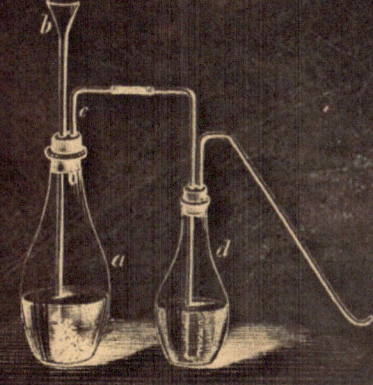

Preparing hydrogen.

Victorian Haiku #129

elixir or no
medicinal properties
raise bottle to lips

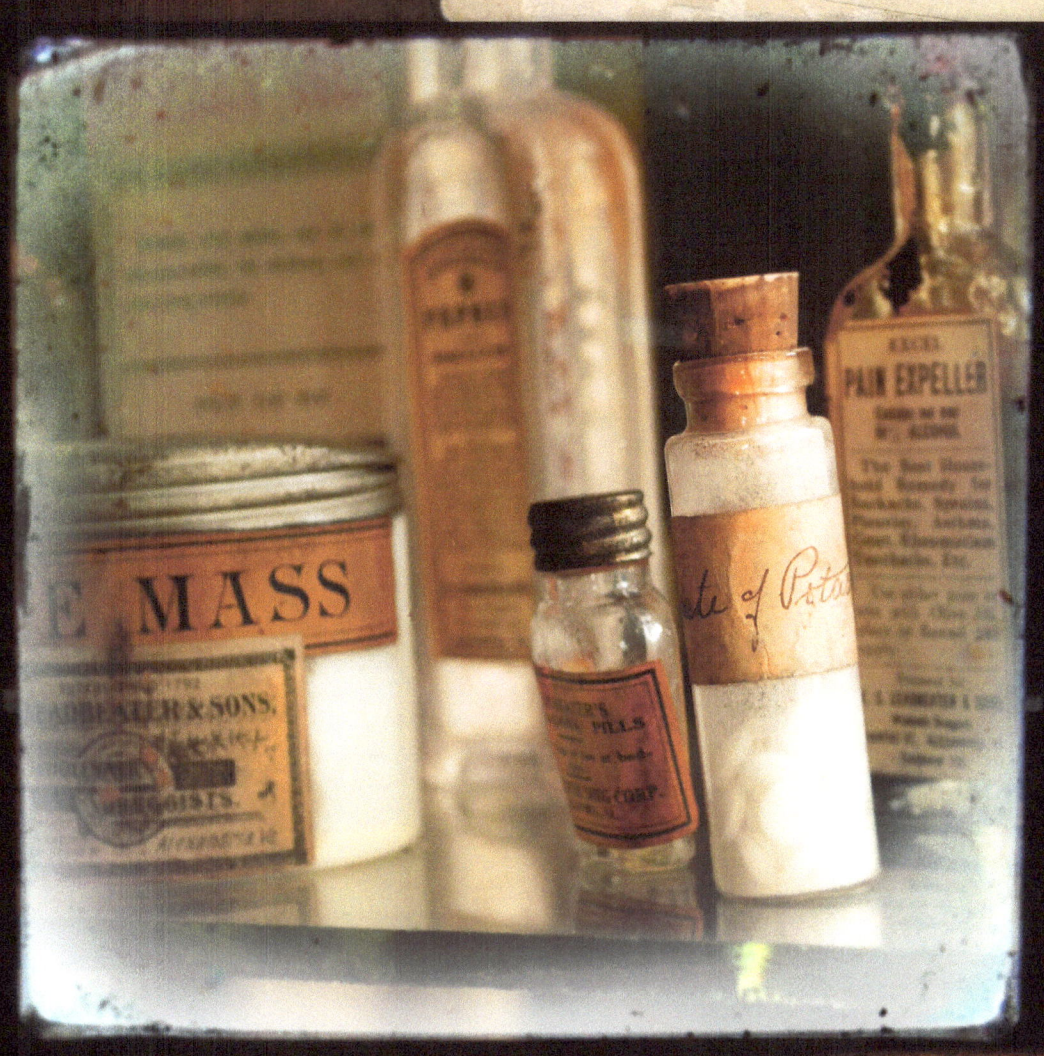

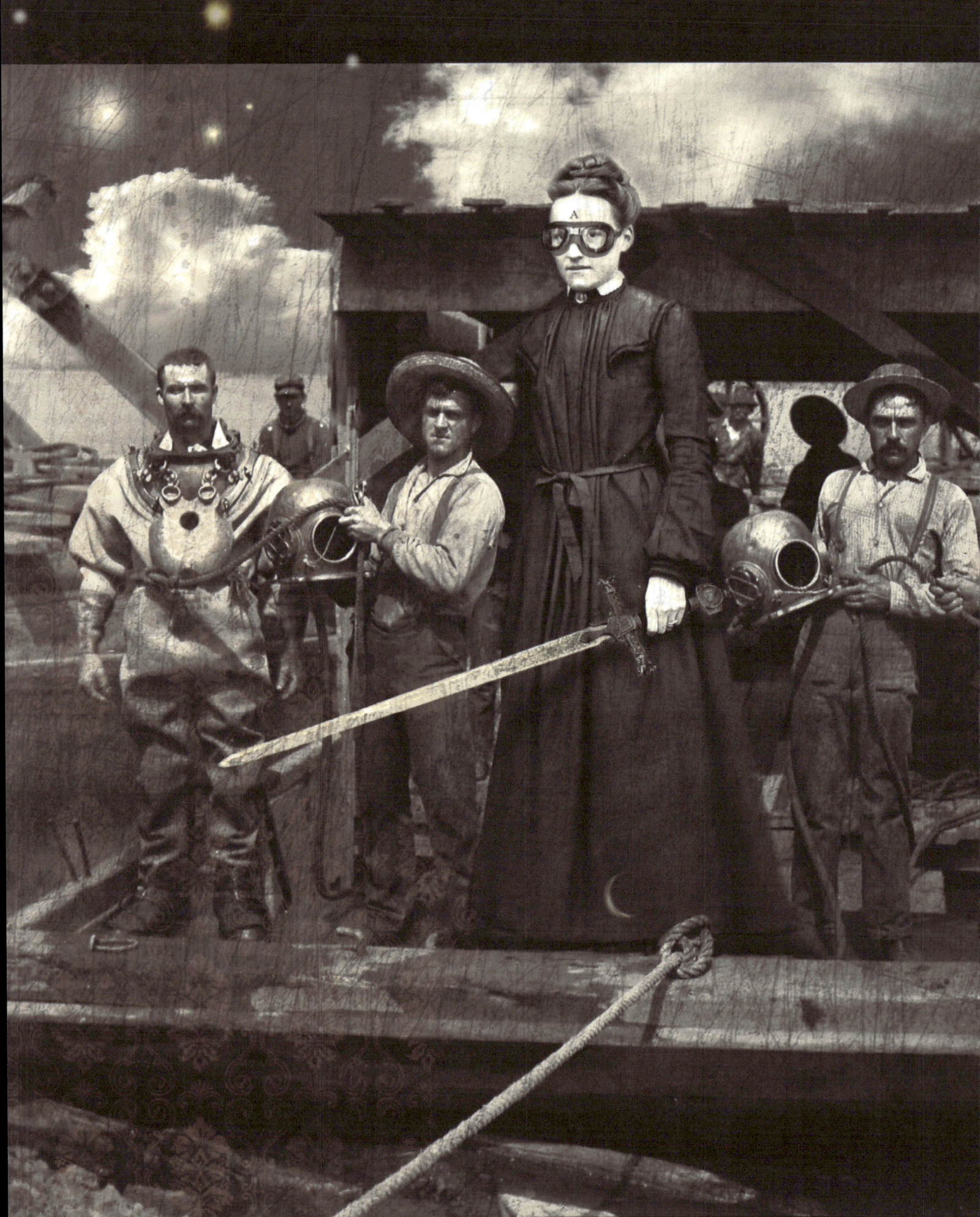

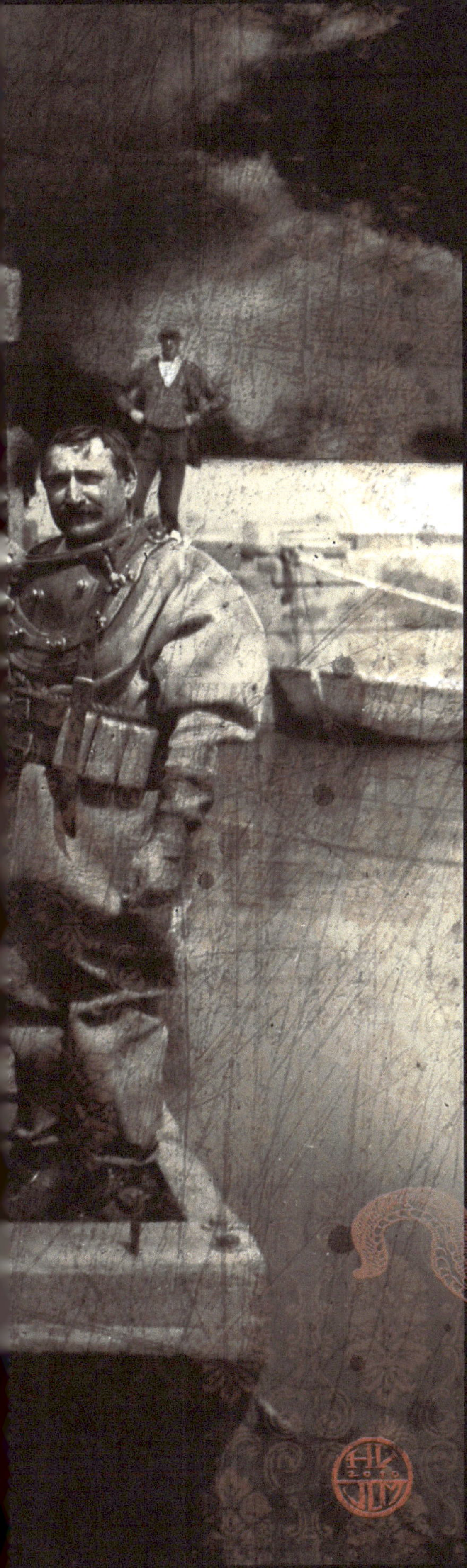

The Lady
Of The Lake

On rare occasions when crossing through the mists, there were accidents—collisions with other boats due to low visibility, bodies overboard as a result of reckless horseplay, etc. Always, the team was assembled to recover the lost, and always she insisted on leading the missions. They were patient and tolerant despite her doing nothing more than standing proudly in the very front of the boat, swinging her sword dangerously in all directions, and chanting, *"viva Avalon!"*

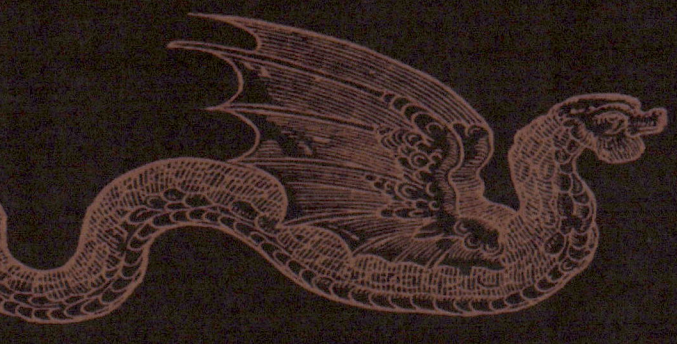

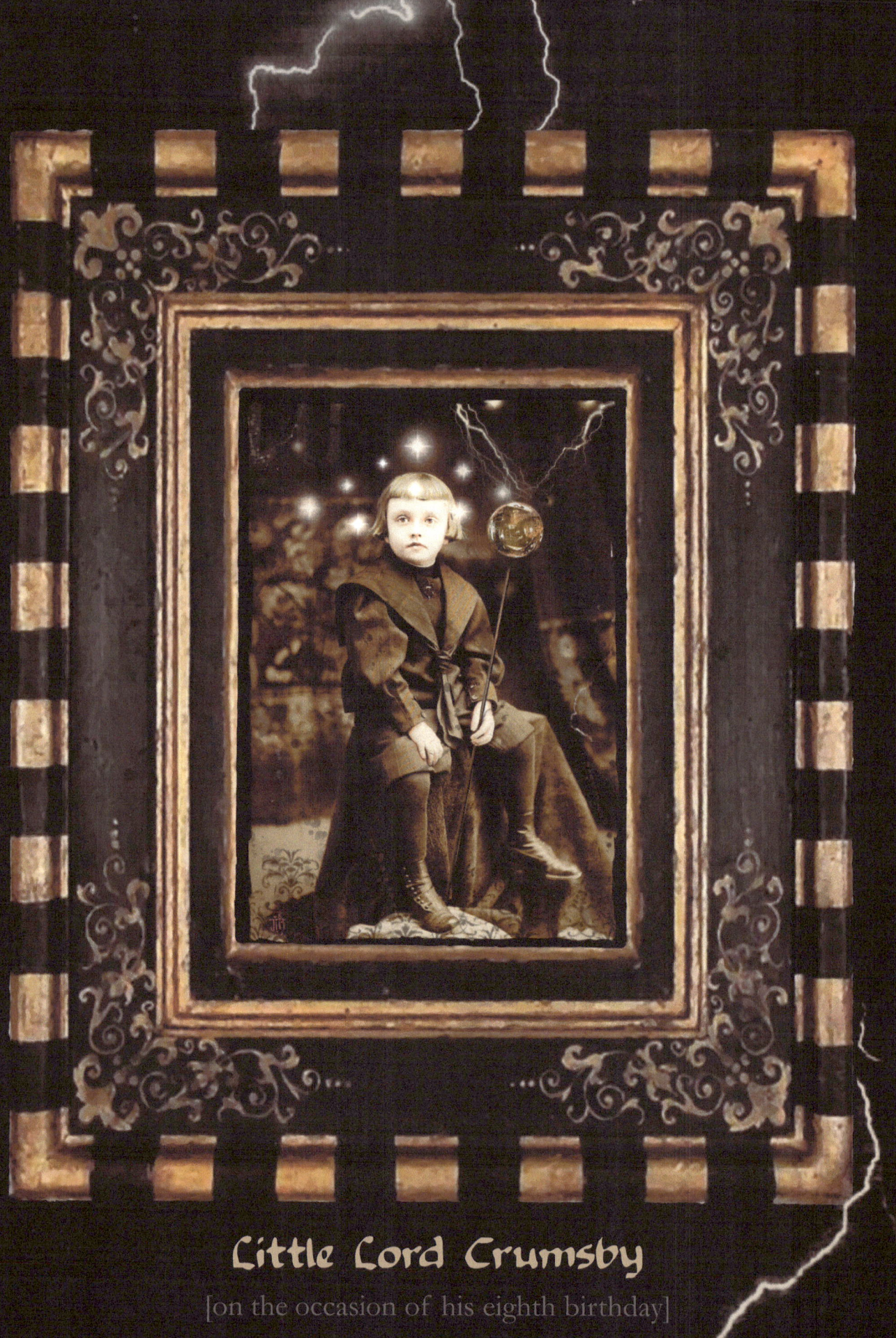

Little Lord Crumsby

[on the occasion of his eighth birthday]

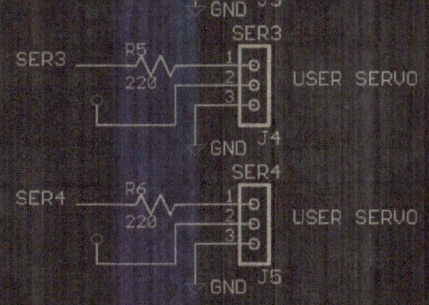

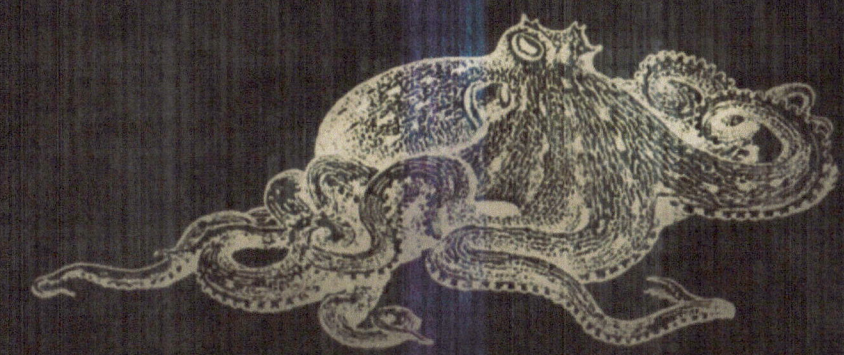

Apothecary.

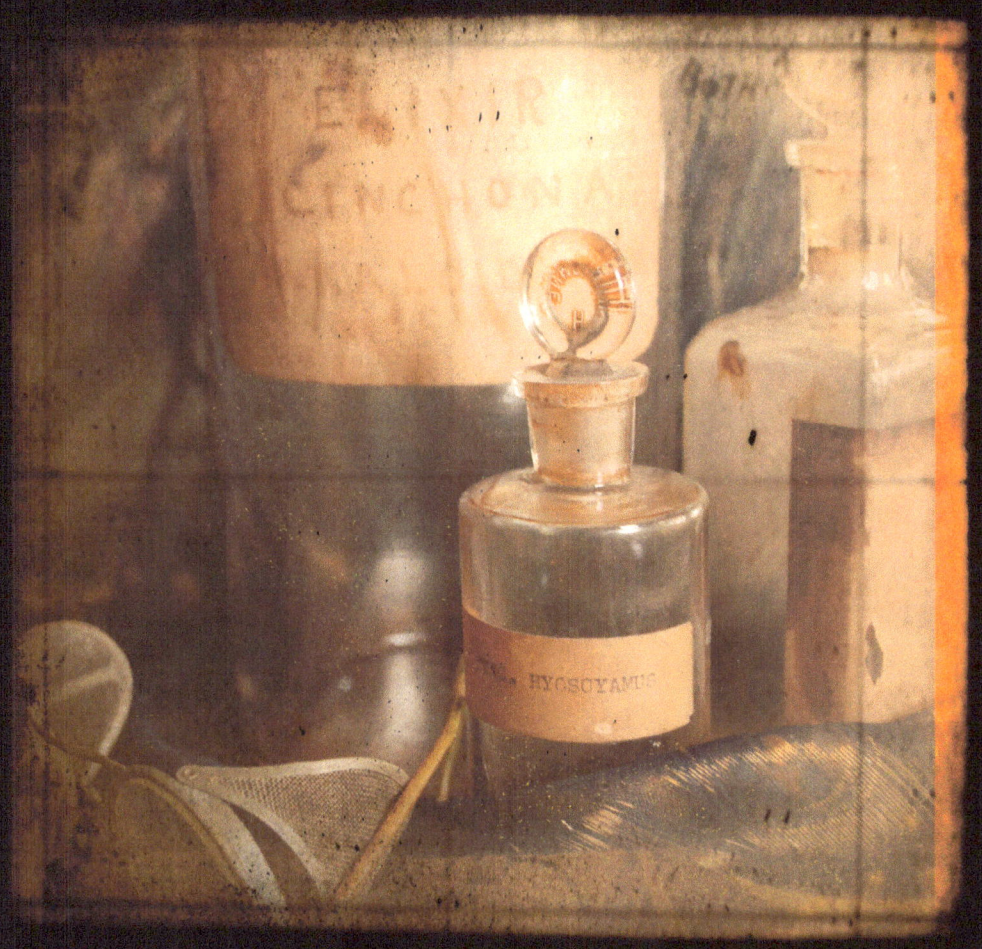

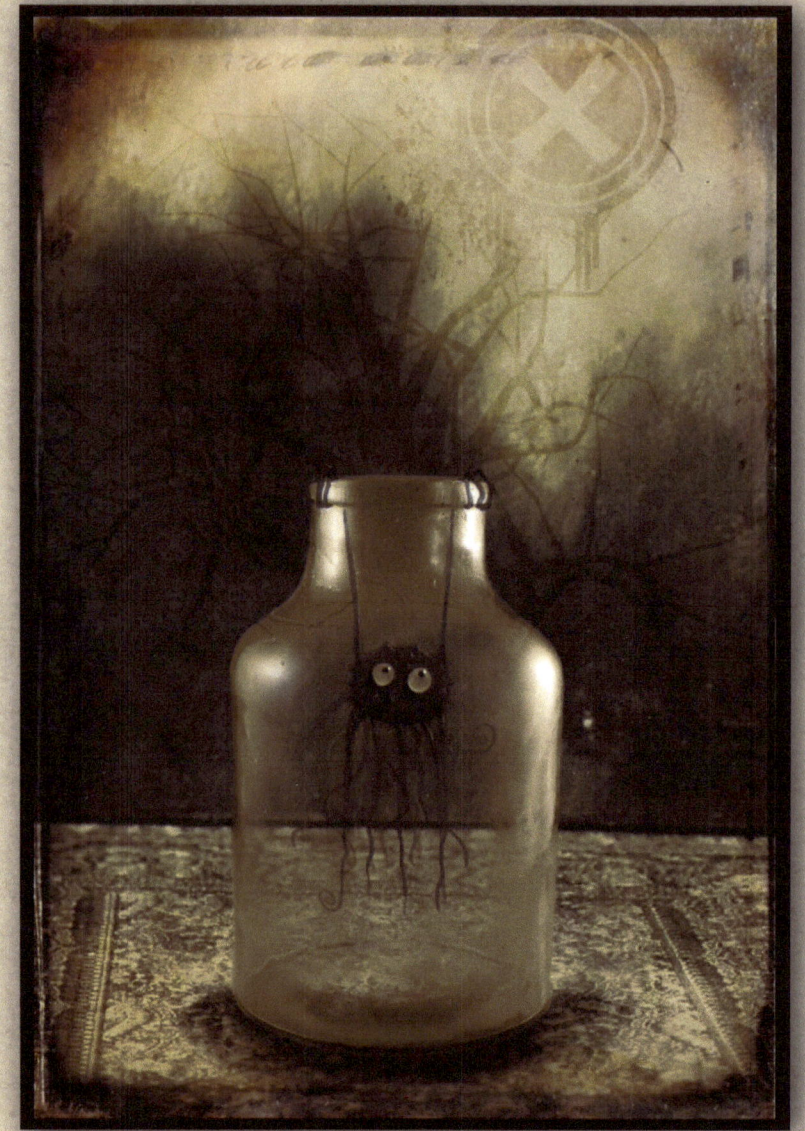

Adenine

Thymine

Guanine

Cytosine

A Most Reluctant Specimen

Fig. 5.

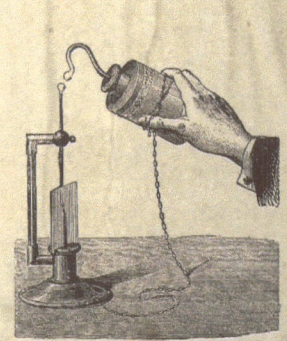

Fig. 1. Percement d'une carte au moyen d'une bouteille
de Leyde.

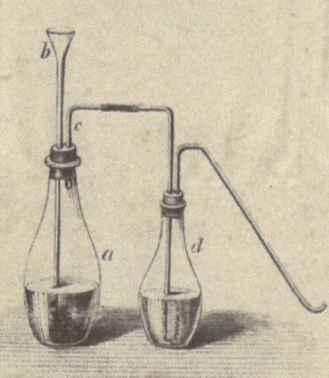

Preparing hydrogen.

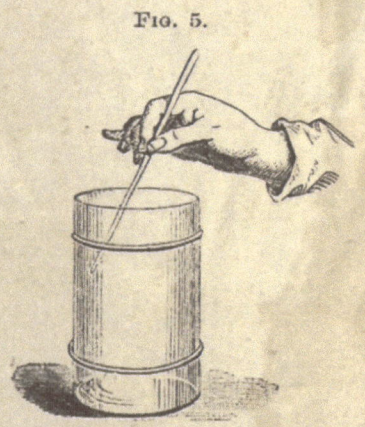

Testing ozone.

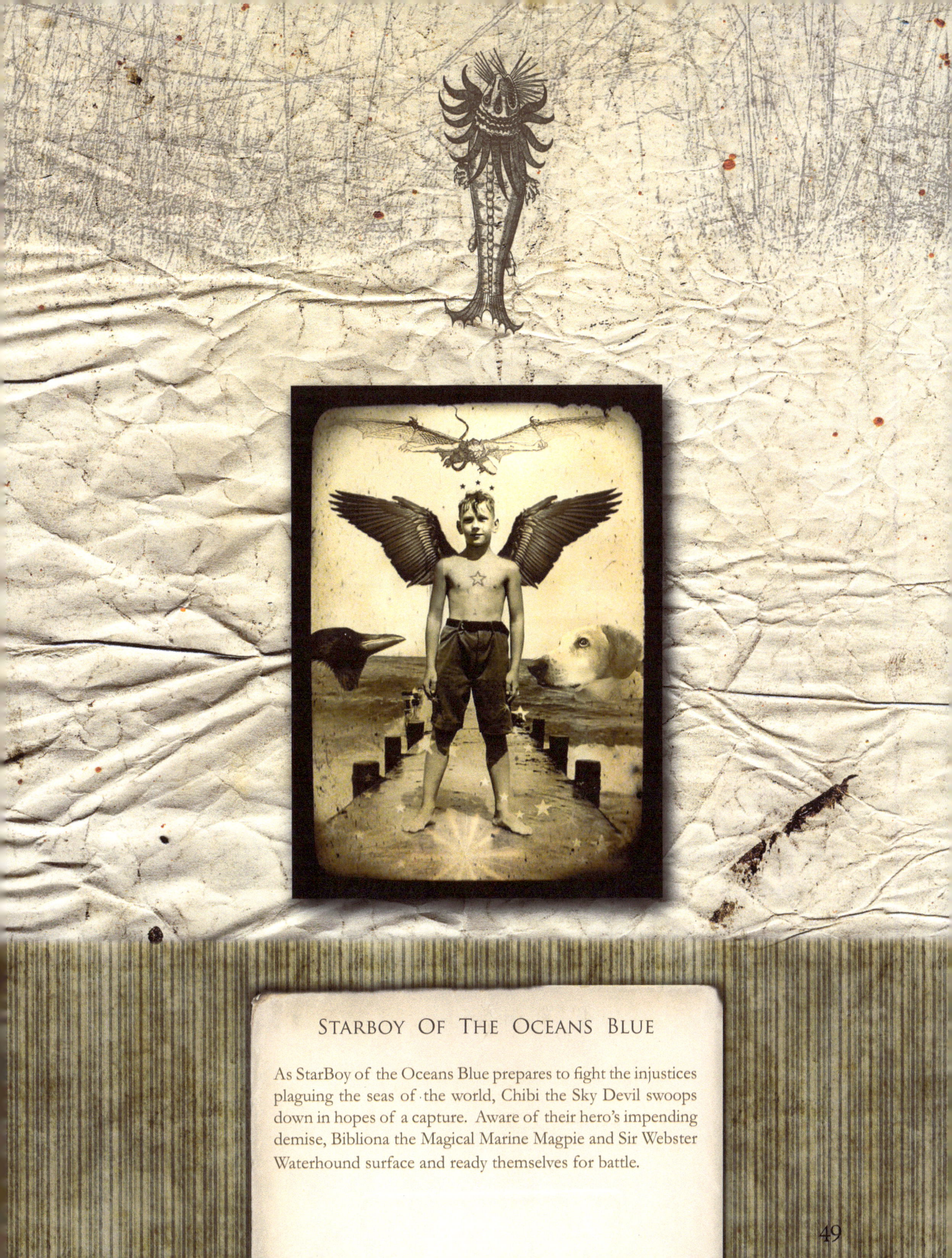

STARBOY OF THE OCEANS BLUE

As StarBoy of the Oceans Blue prepares to fight the injustices plaguing the seas of the world, Chibi the Sky Devil swoops down in hopes of a capture. Aware of their hero's impending demise, Bibliona the Magical Marine Magpie and Sir Webster Waterhound surface and ready themselves for battle.

THE LOWER DEAD HORSE

FALL FESTIVAL

and

NONCHALANT BALANCING COMPETITION
of 1892

* * * * * *

"I CAN DO THIS. I CAN DO THIS. I'VE BEEN

UP HERE EACH OF THE LAST 322 YEARS.

IT SHOULD COME EASY BY NOW.

JUST...NEED...TO FOCUS."

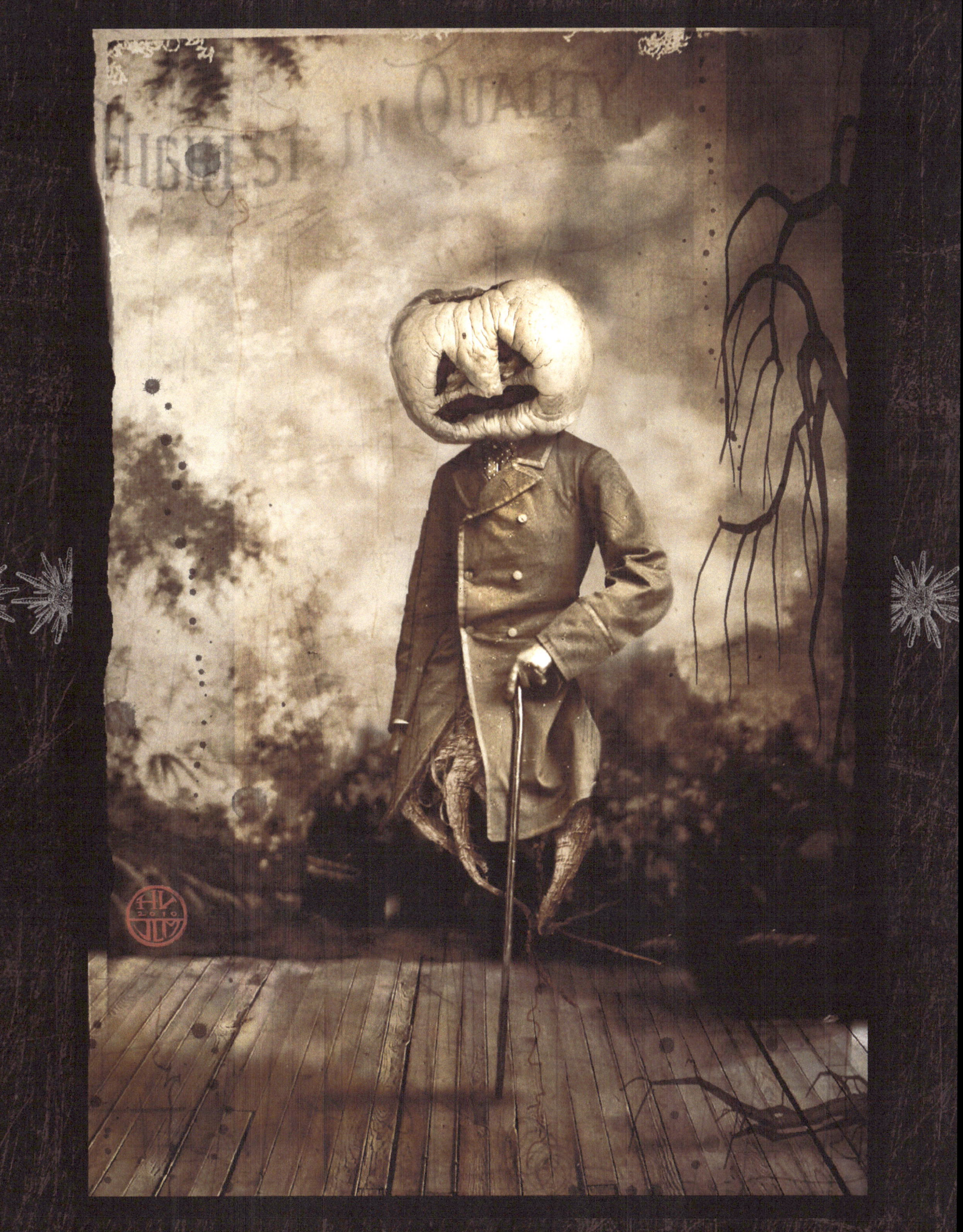

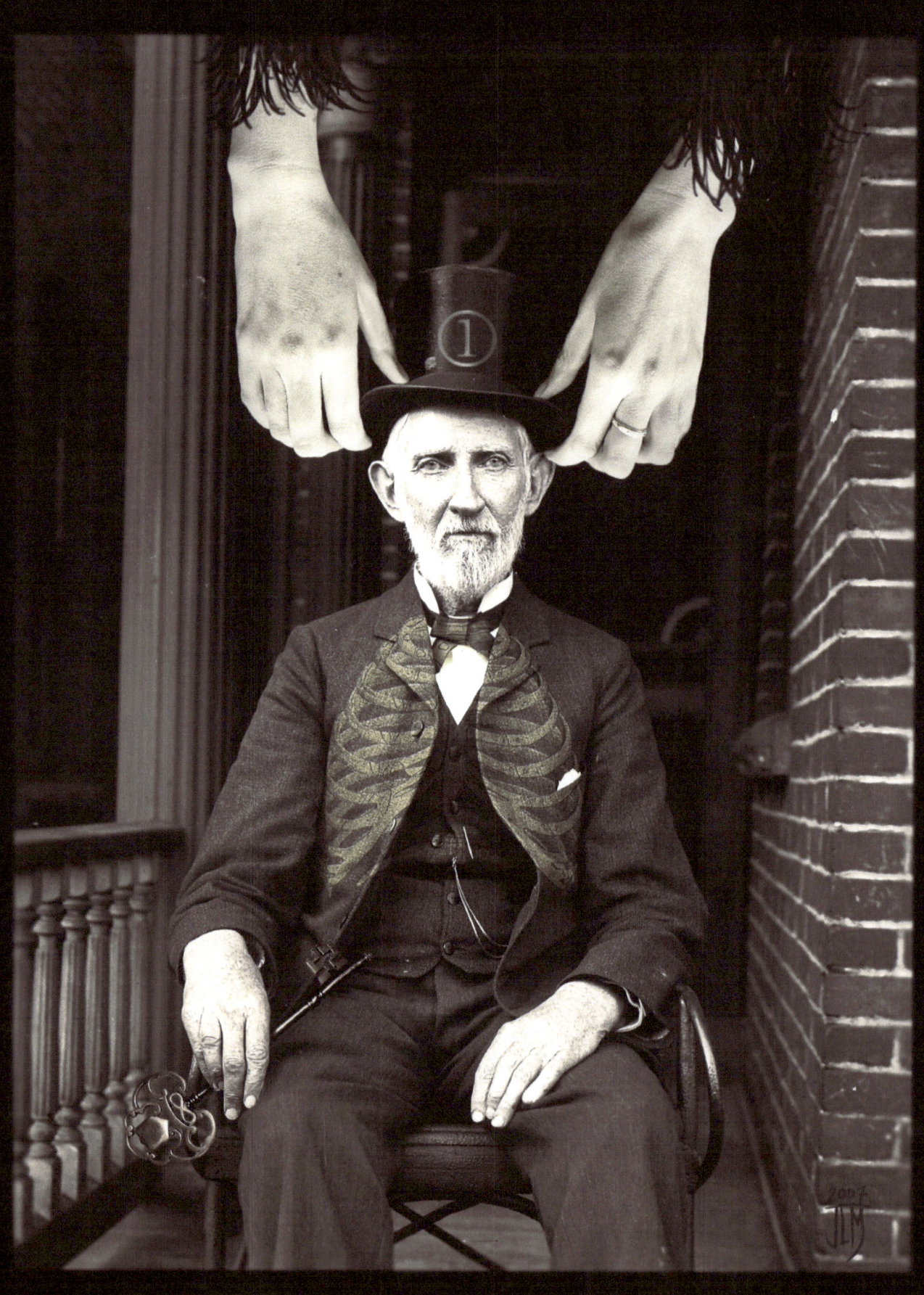

Masonic Rite 201.
promotion from on high

52

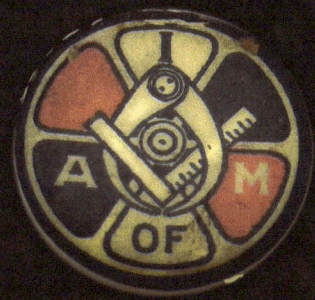

201

Thaddeus T. Gorman, already showing
off the key to the city of Pittsburgh
(few people realize it was gated as
late as 1962) and a top coat made
especially for him by the National
Embalming and Crematoria Research
Organisation, both of which he received
in 1874 for outstanding funerary and
security services.

A known compatriot of Emperor Joshua
Norton I of America, General Custer,
Harry Houdini and Dr. Joseph Bell,
Gorman was not present in London in 1888,
nor San Francisco in 1906.

He died in 1948 and again in 1952.

Narrative by Jamie Ward-Brown

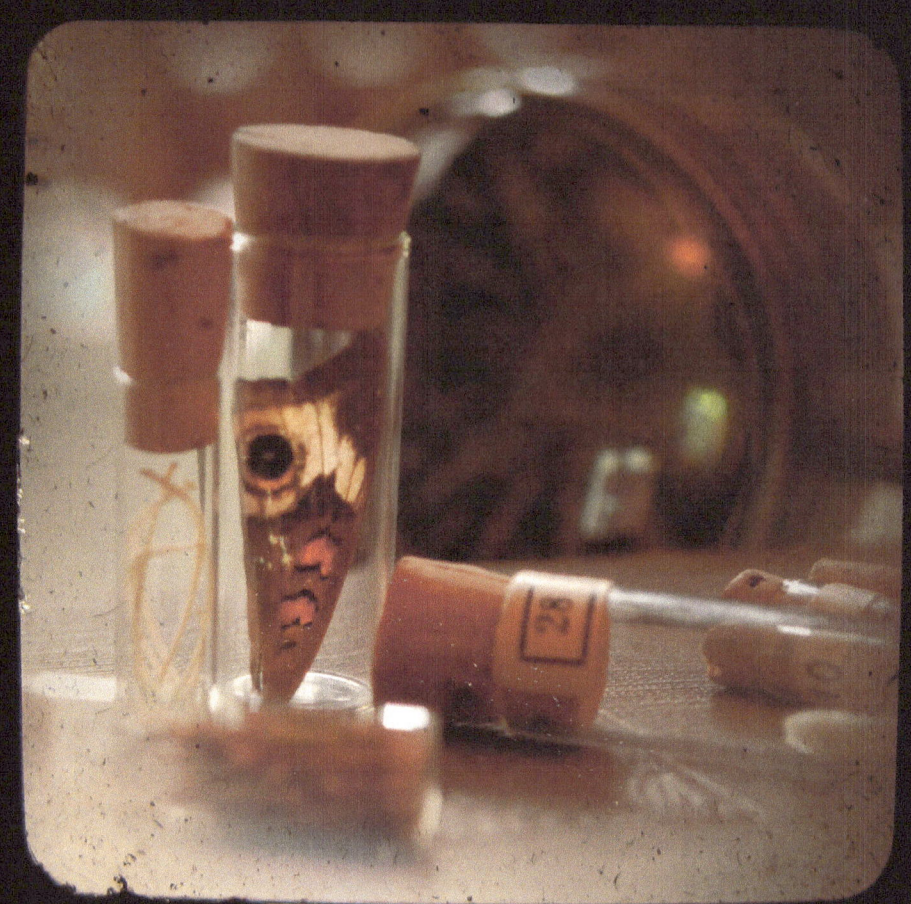

Light Through Wing

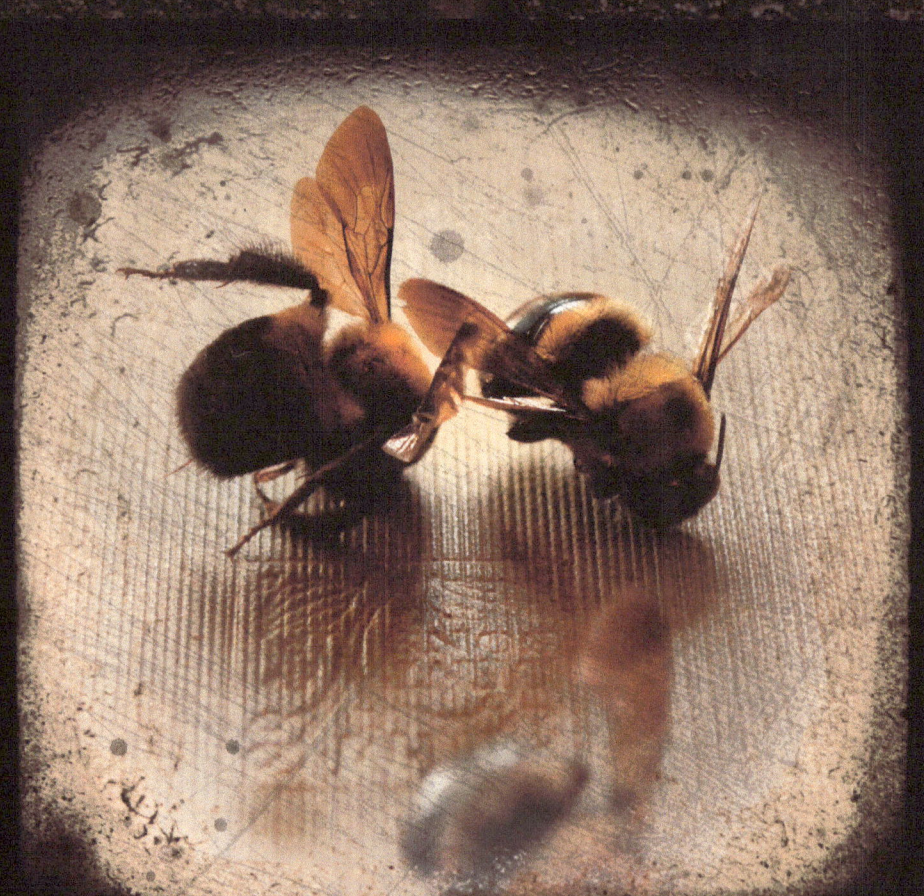

Ex-bee Dance

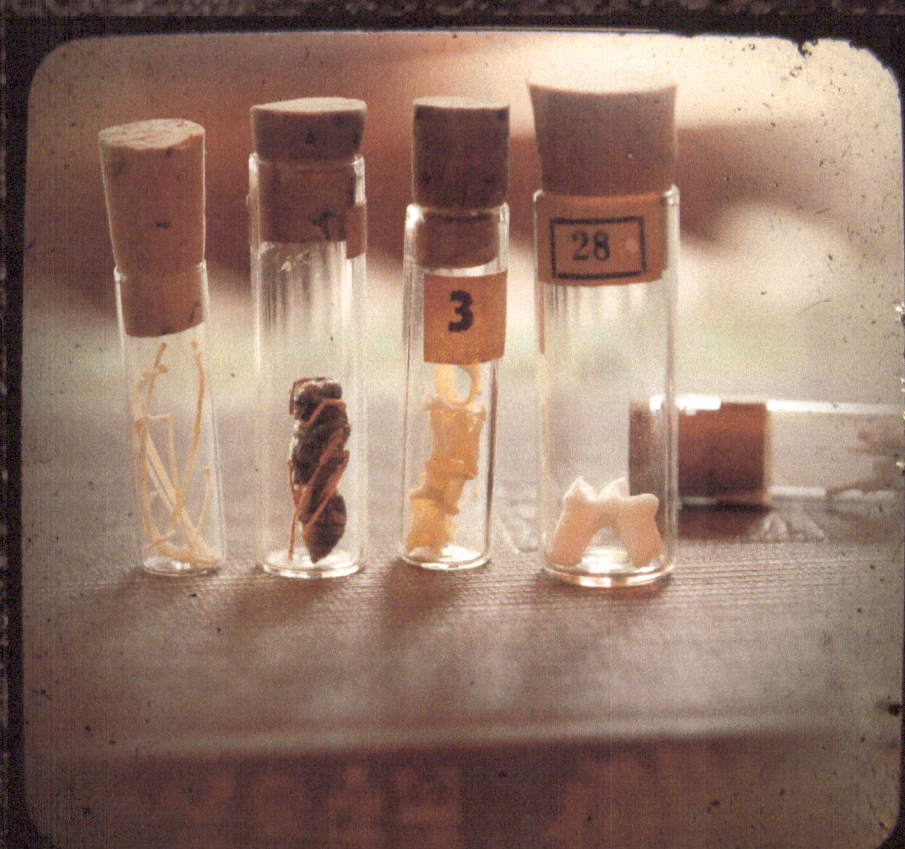

Collection

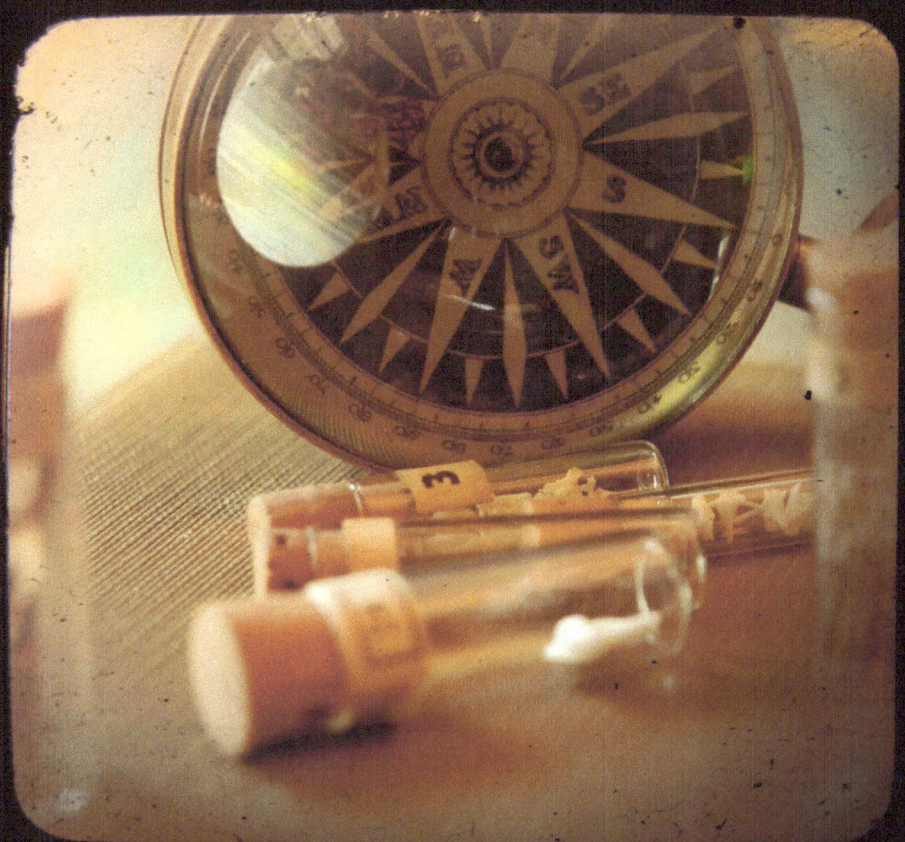

Compass and Specimens

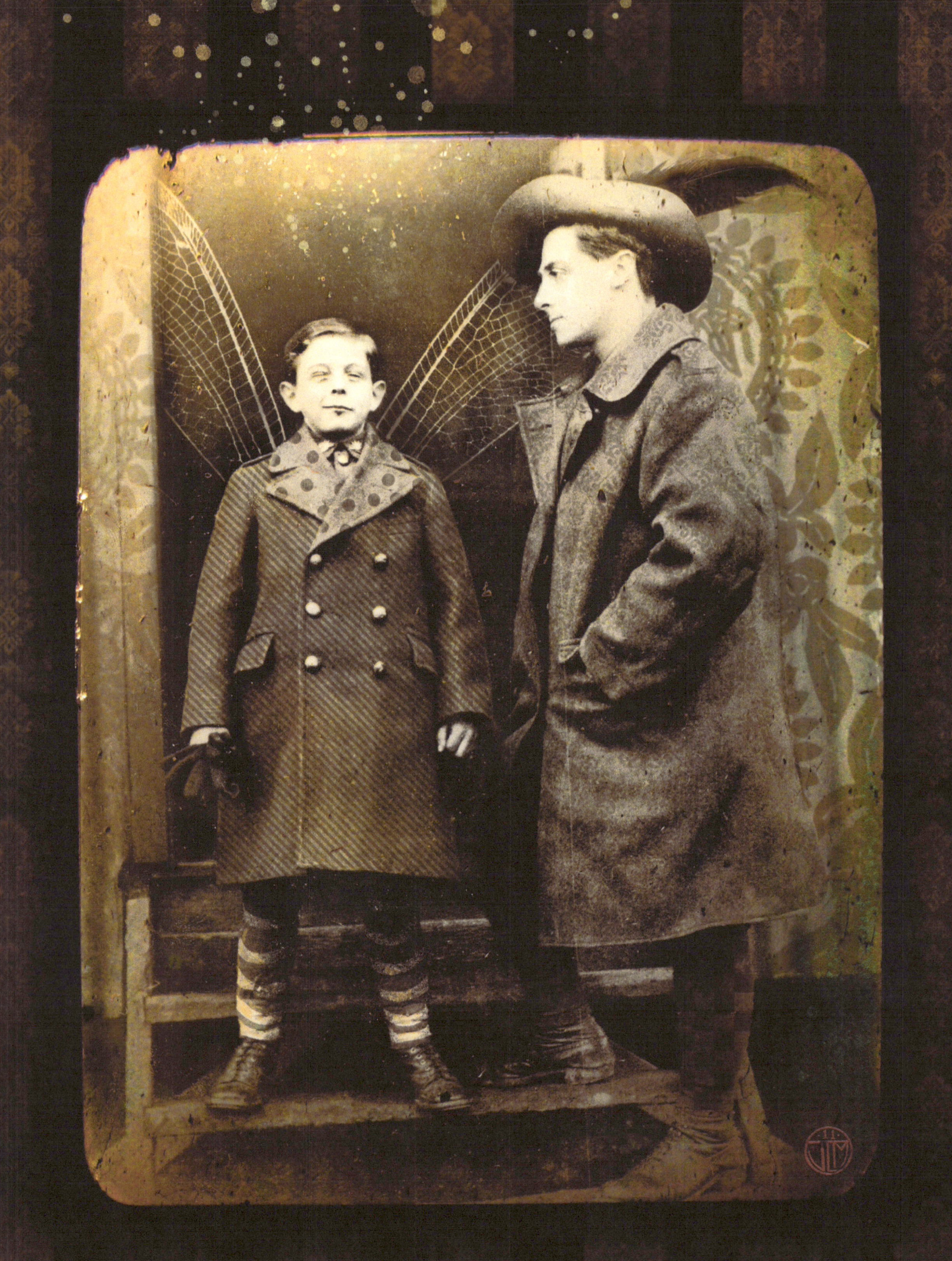

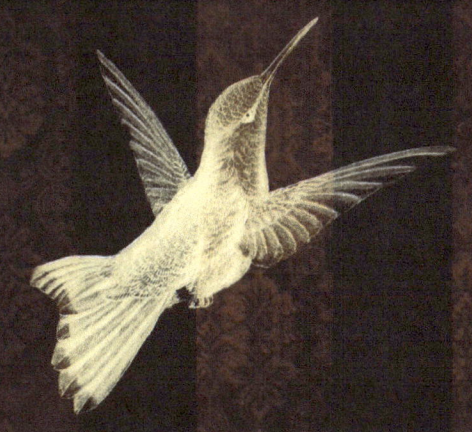

A Watchful Eye

Once his wings were fully formed Danny Fly puffed out his chest and exuded a confidence like he never had before. Yes, he was a sideshow, and yes, people were skeptical of his dragonfly-like wings. But to Danny it mattered not. He knew who he was, and he wanted nothing more than to take flight and show them all, but knew he was under the close supervision of his older brother at all times. He'd wait till the time was right. He could wait.

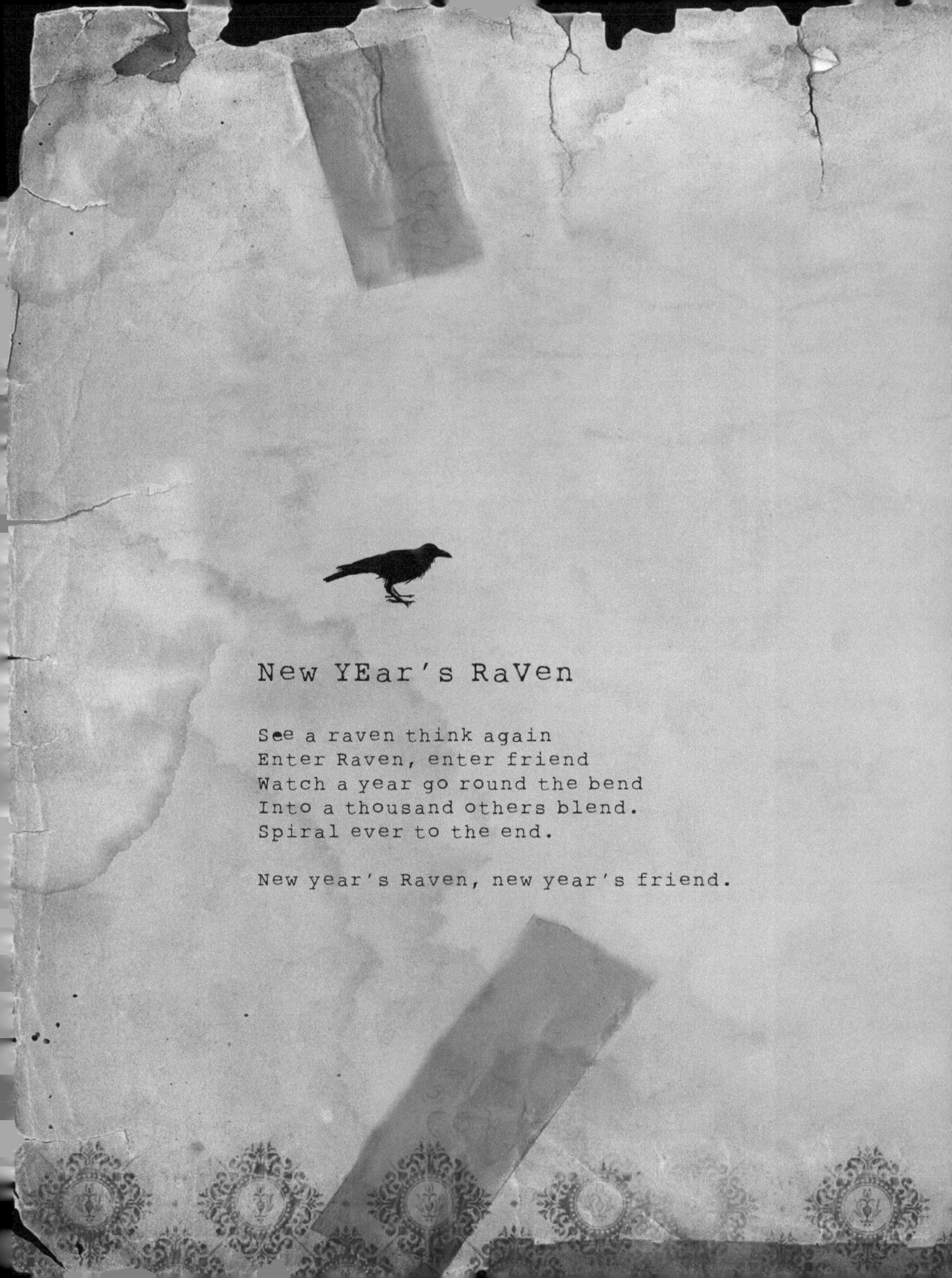

New YEar's RaVen

See a raven think again
Enter Raven, enter friend
Watch a year go round the bend
Into a thousand others blend.
Spiral ever to the end.

New year's Raven, new year's friend.

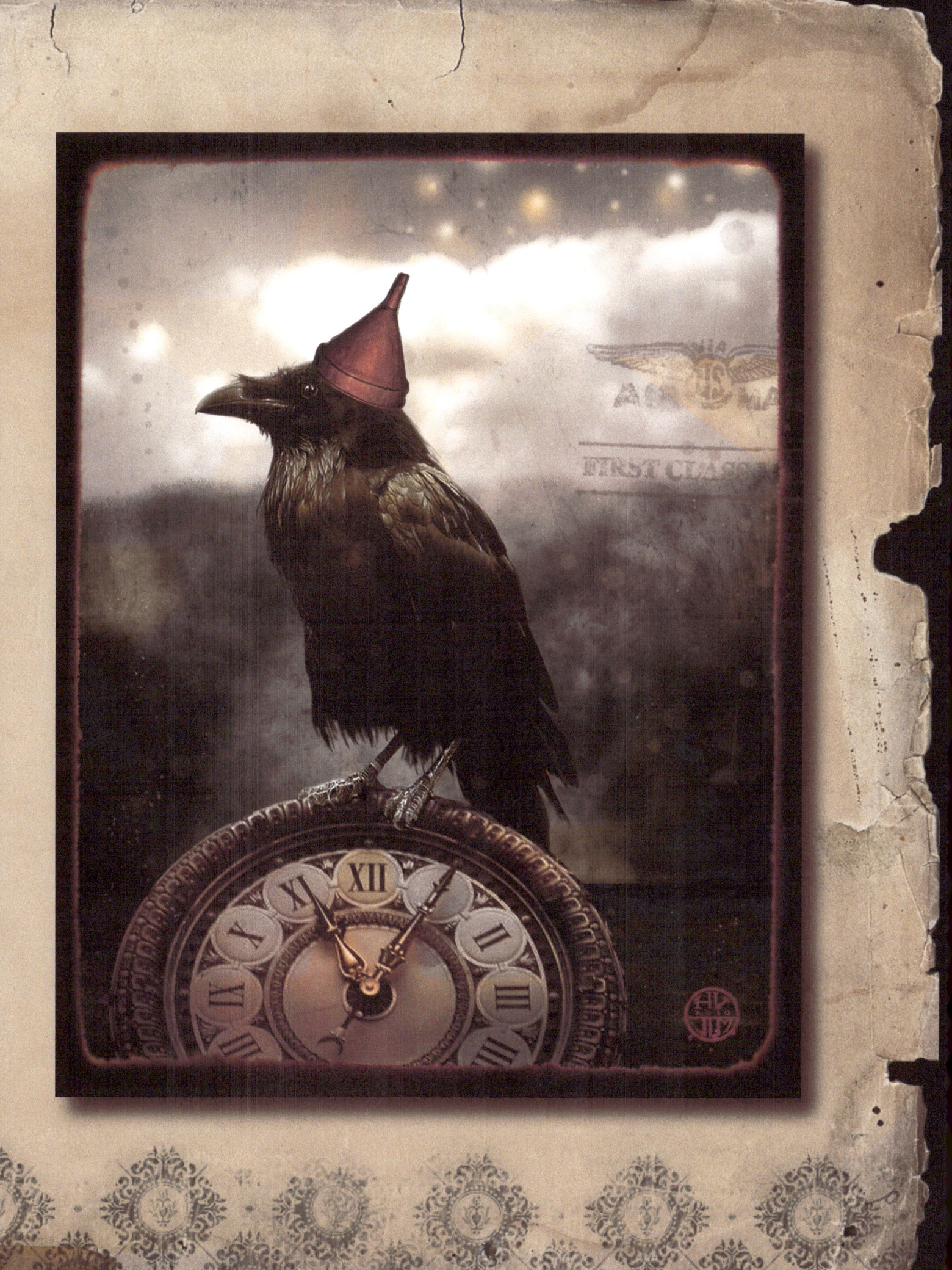

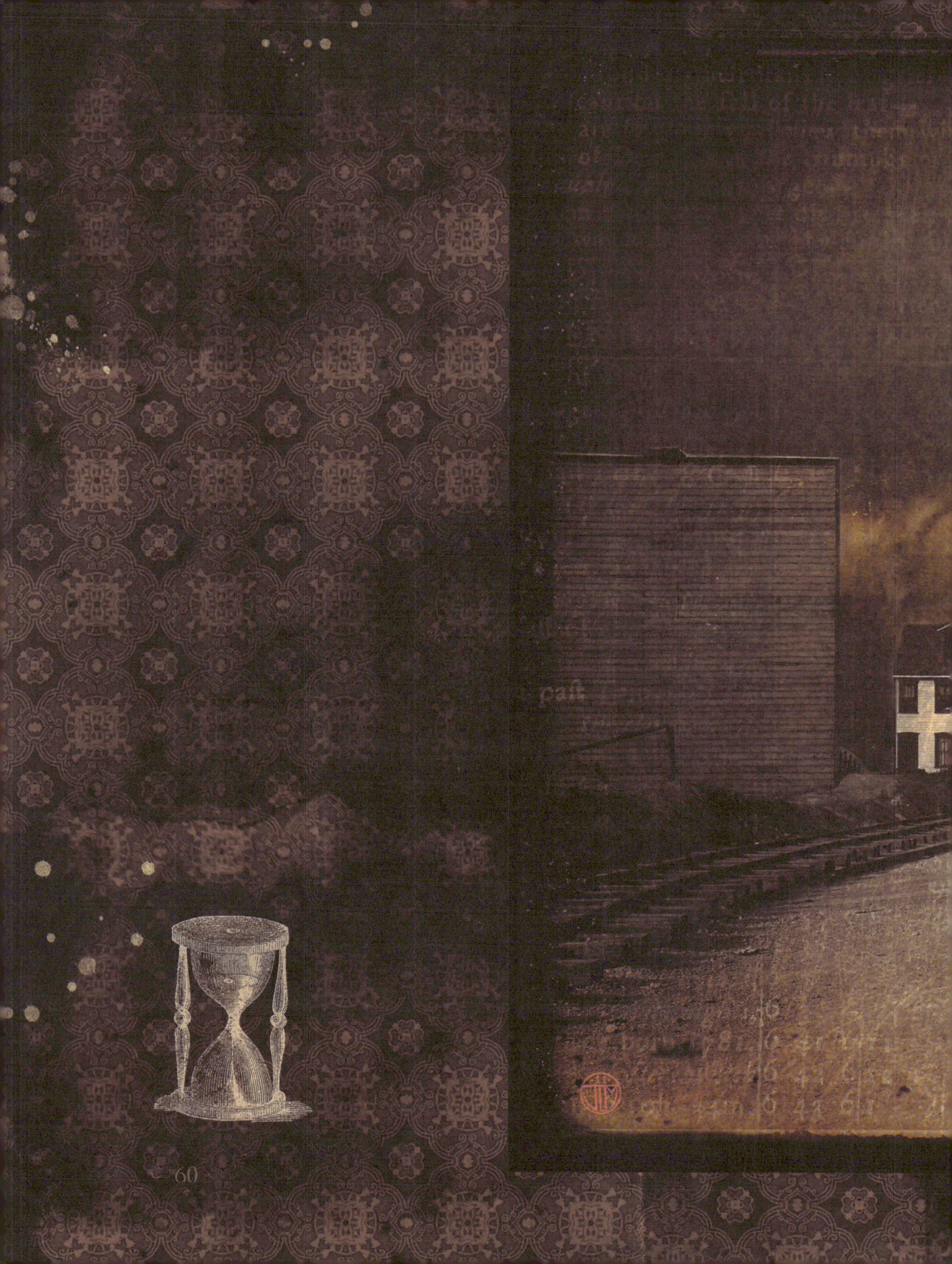

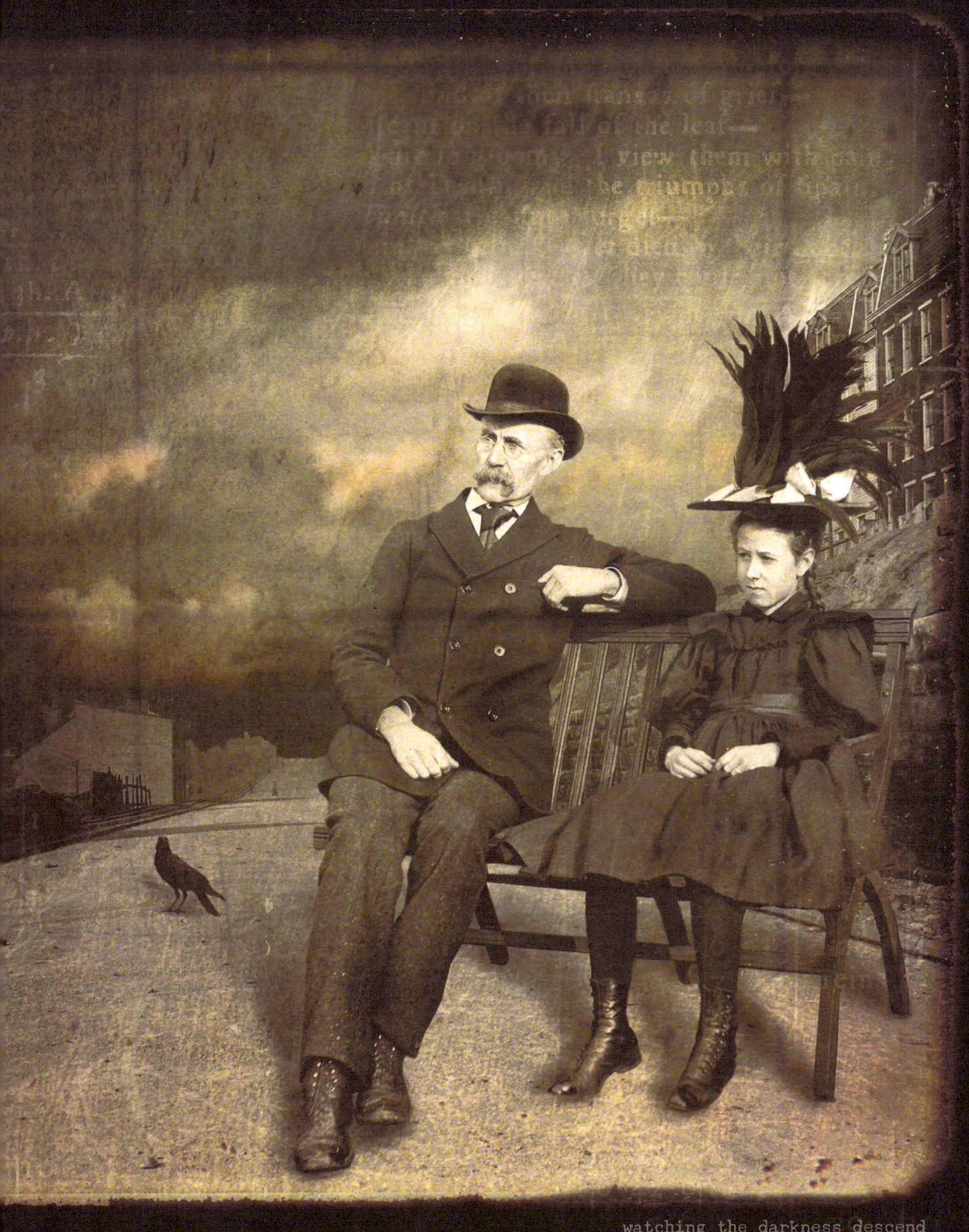

watching the darkness descend

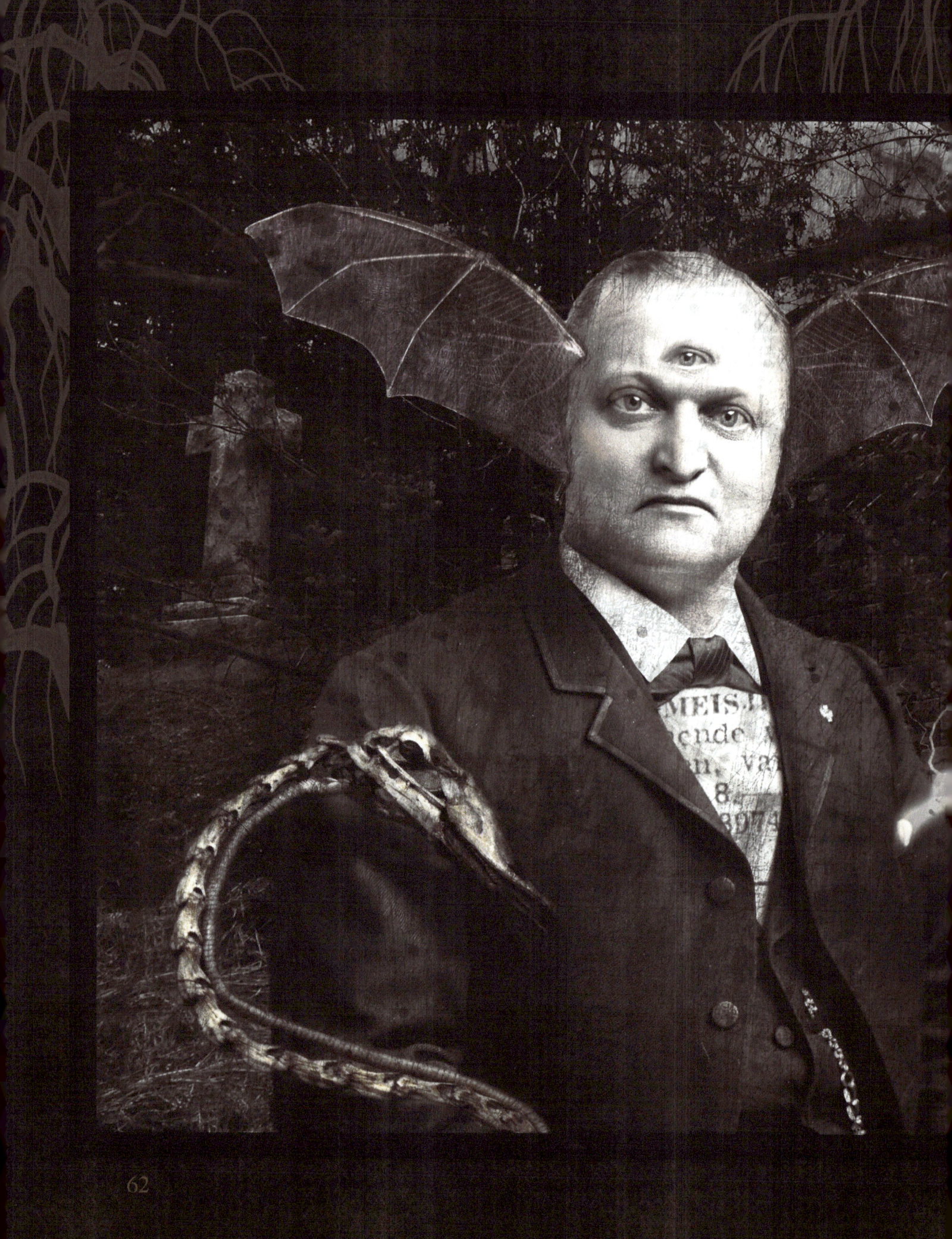

THE ONE TRUE PUMPKIN KING

Behold, His Holiness the Bahbra Binki's evil twin brother, Gerald. Although he developed a true third eye, it would be forever sightless, while Binki, in a spiritual sense, saw with his through all of time and space.

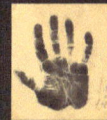

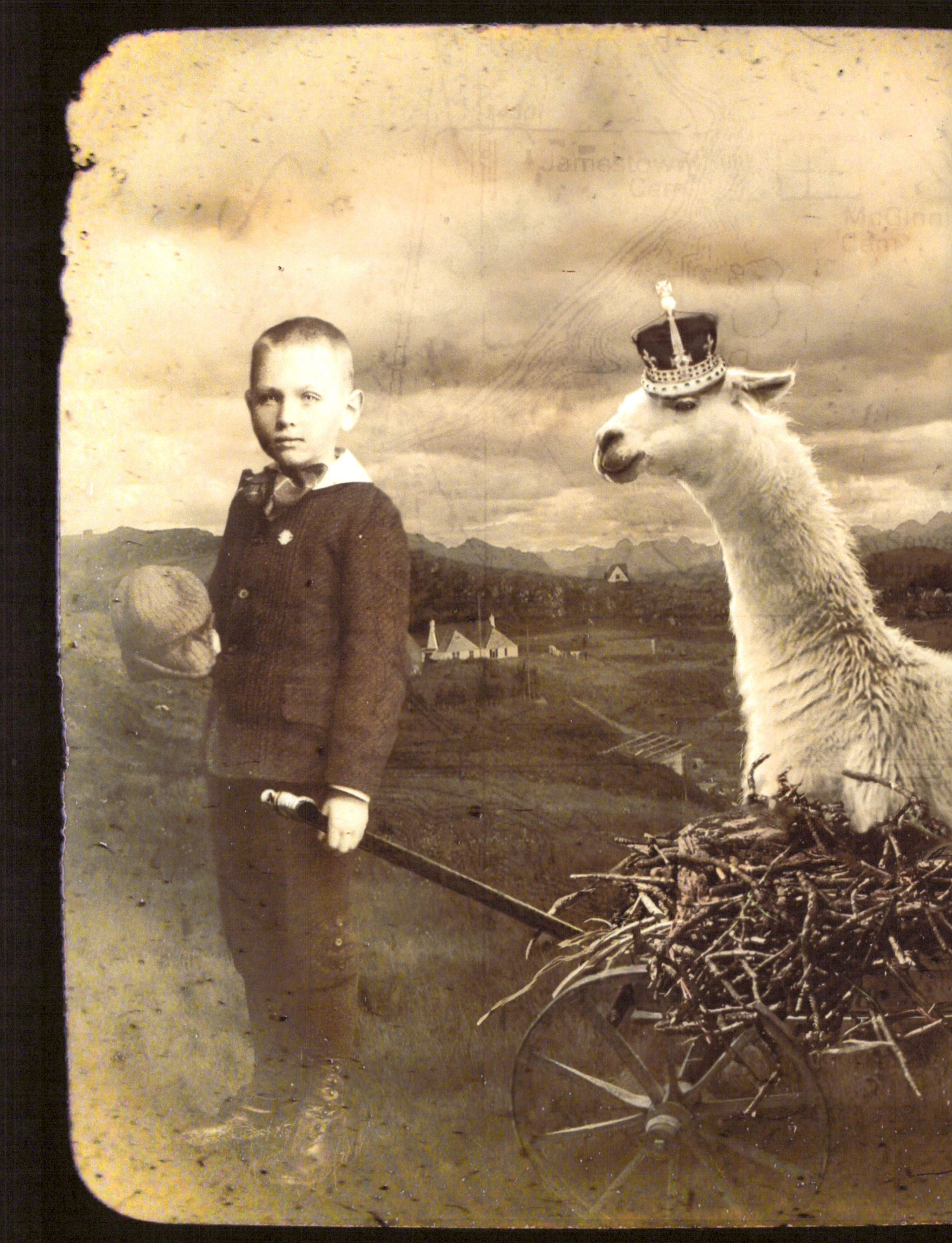

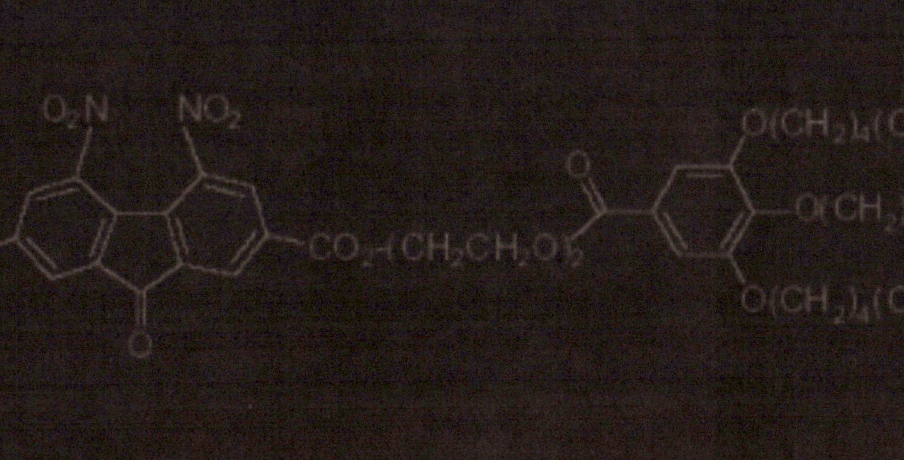

McLEGGIN AND THE WHITE QUEEN

Young Sorrow McLeggin of John O'Groats set out to see if any osprey had taken up residence in the haphazard twig nests he'd built for his school science fair project. To his amazement, a beautiful, white llama was found to be lazily inhabiting one of the nests. How she got there he'd no idea, but adopt her as his own he did. After all, she was not just any llama, she was the White Queen—most rare indeed. He was awarded the Rupert T. Harrowsby Prize for Primary School Science Genius in 1904 and went on to first imagine antimatter, though he kept the dark dream completely to himself. He died in 1954, after a tragic accident in which he impaled his foot with his own walking stick and died of sepsis a fortnight later. His journals filled with his scientific ramblings were found behind a moldering loaf of bread in his ice box.

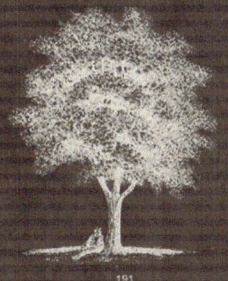

THE BLADE

IN NORSE MYTHOLOGY, THE GOD ODIN WAS KNOWN AS THE RAVEN GOD, BECAUSE HE KEPT TWO RAVENS AS MESSENGERS, huginn AND muninn. THESE BIRDS WERE SENT OFF EACH DAY TO FLY AROUND THE WORLD TO OBSERVE AND BRING BACK INFORMATION TO ODIN. IT WAS SAID THAT ODIN GAVE HIS TWO RAVENS THE ABILITY TO SPEAK SO THAT THEY COULD KEEP HIM INFORMED ABOUT IMPORTANT EVENTS IN THE WORLD.

huginn IS OLD NORSE FOR "THOUGHT."

Victorian Haiku #77

absinthe, my divine

measured life be gone this night

faerie green, alight

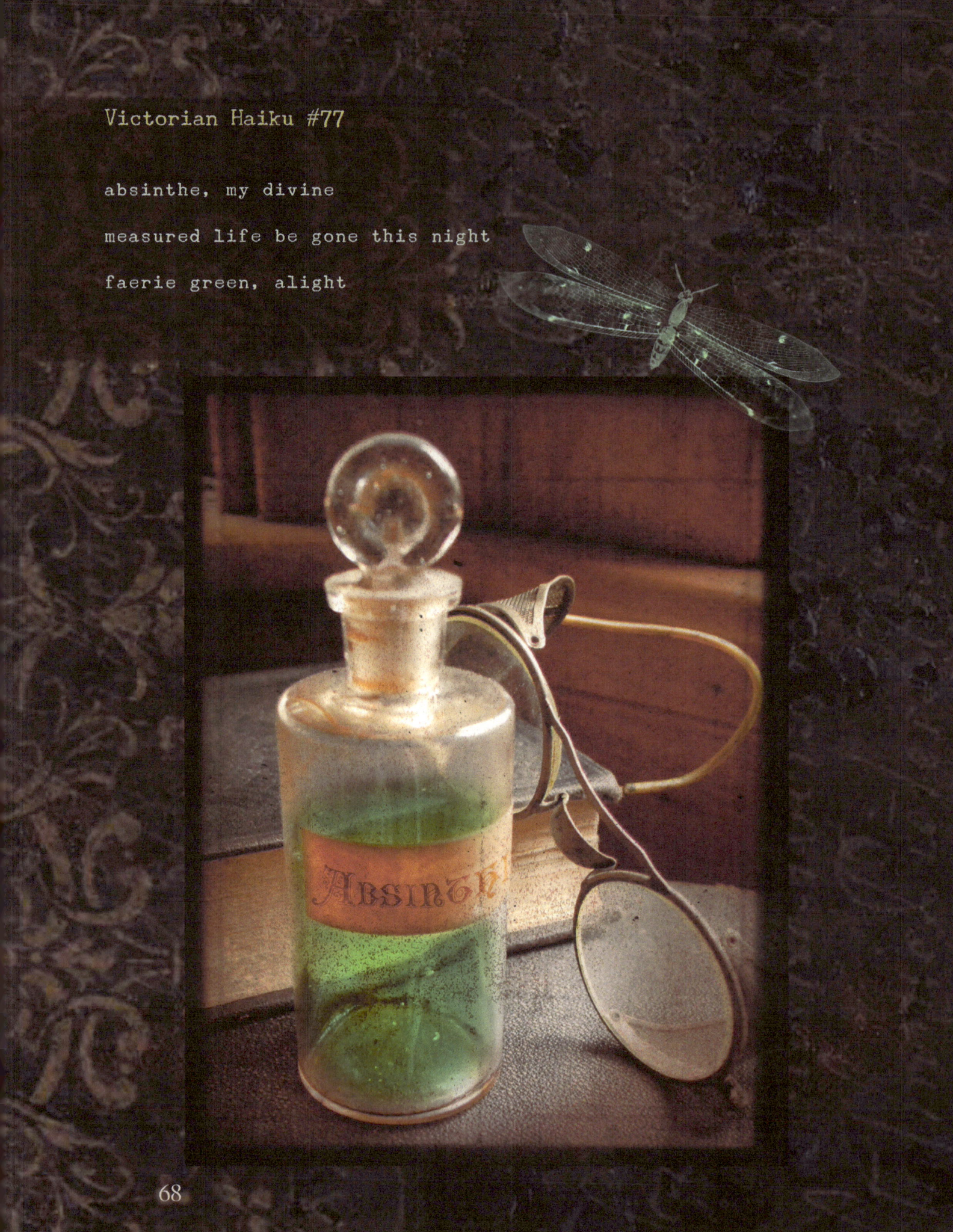

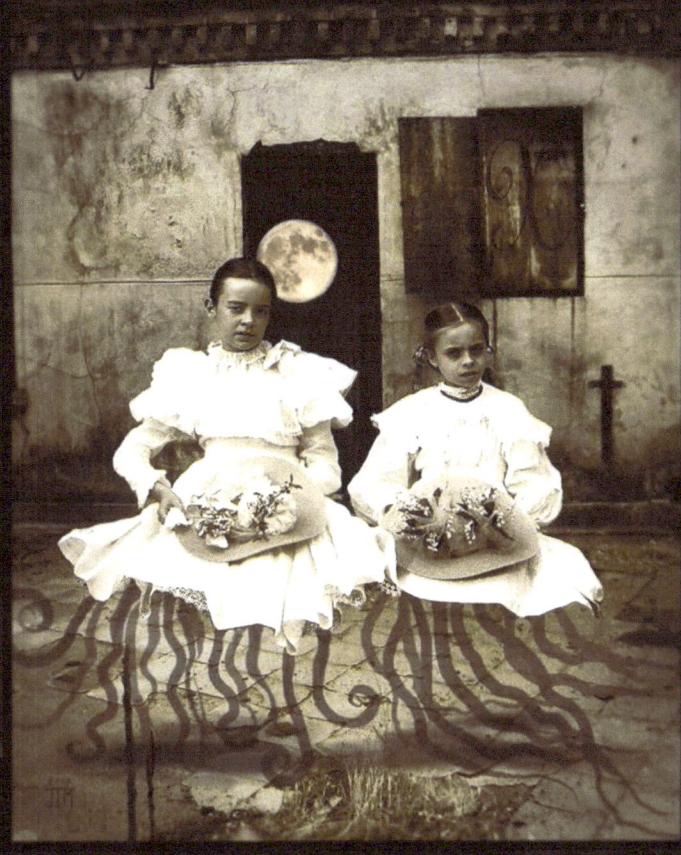

Moonrise Over The Ika Estate

Hair in ribbons, dressed in their finest Sunday clothes they hovered like magic carpets, tentacles barely grazing the ground, outside well past bedtime waiting for the moonrise. Oxa and Nippa chose to face east. Always. But where was the moon? How was it they always missed its shining face?

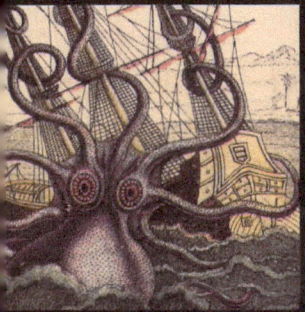

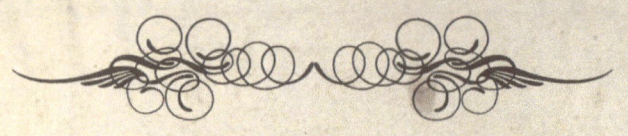

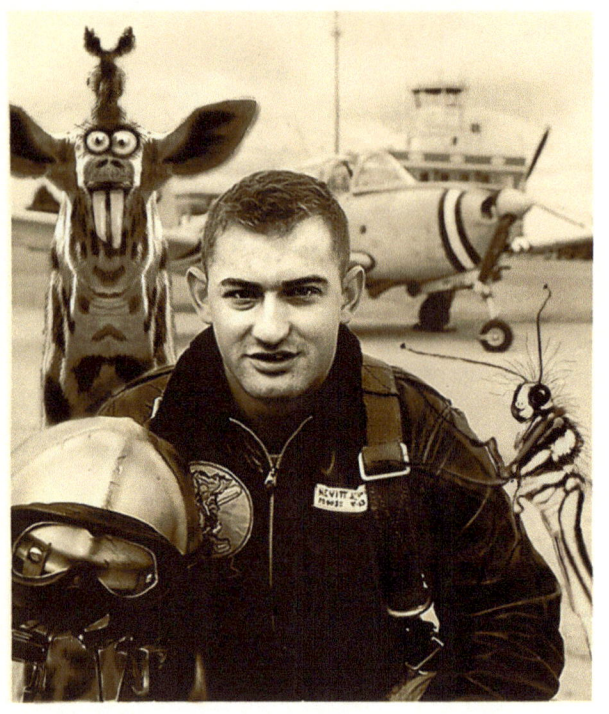

Return From Terra Incognita

He was gone a long time—almost two years longer than the mission was expected to take. Family and friends assumed he had been lost in the wilds never to be seen again. Surprising them all on an overcast day in April, his plane landed at the base. It was too quiet; the others present reported that no engine could be heard. He stepped down from the craft, smiling but with a distant and detached look in his eyes. All appeared well. He seemed happy, healthy and hadn't aged a day. His uniform showed no signs of wear and tear as any garment should after having been worn continuously for so long. He had not lost weight. He would not speak.

Then behind him appeared two other forms. He had brought back with him some new friends.

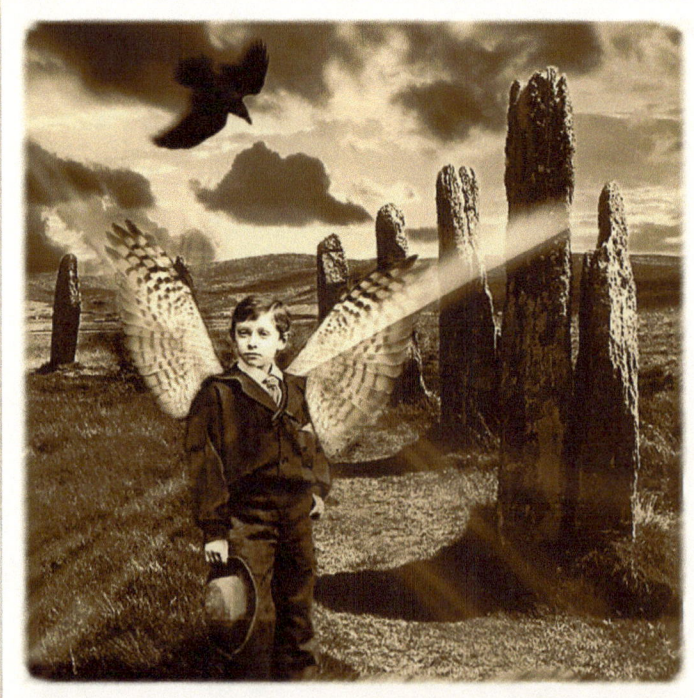

An Angel Descends in Orkney

Winter solstice morning, 1841, an angel appears inside the Ring of Brodgar, Mainland, Orkney, Scotland.

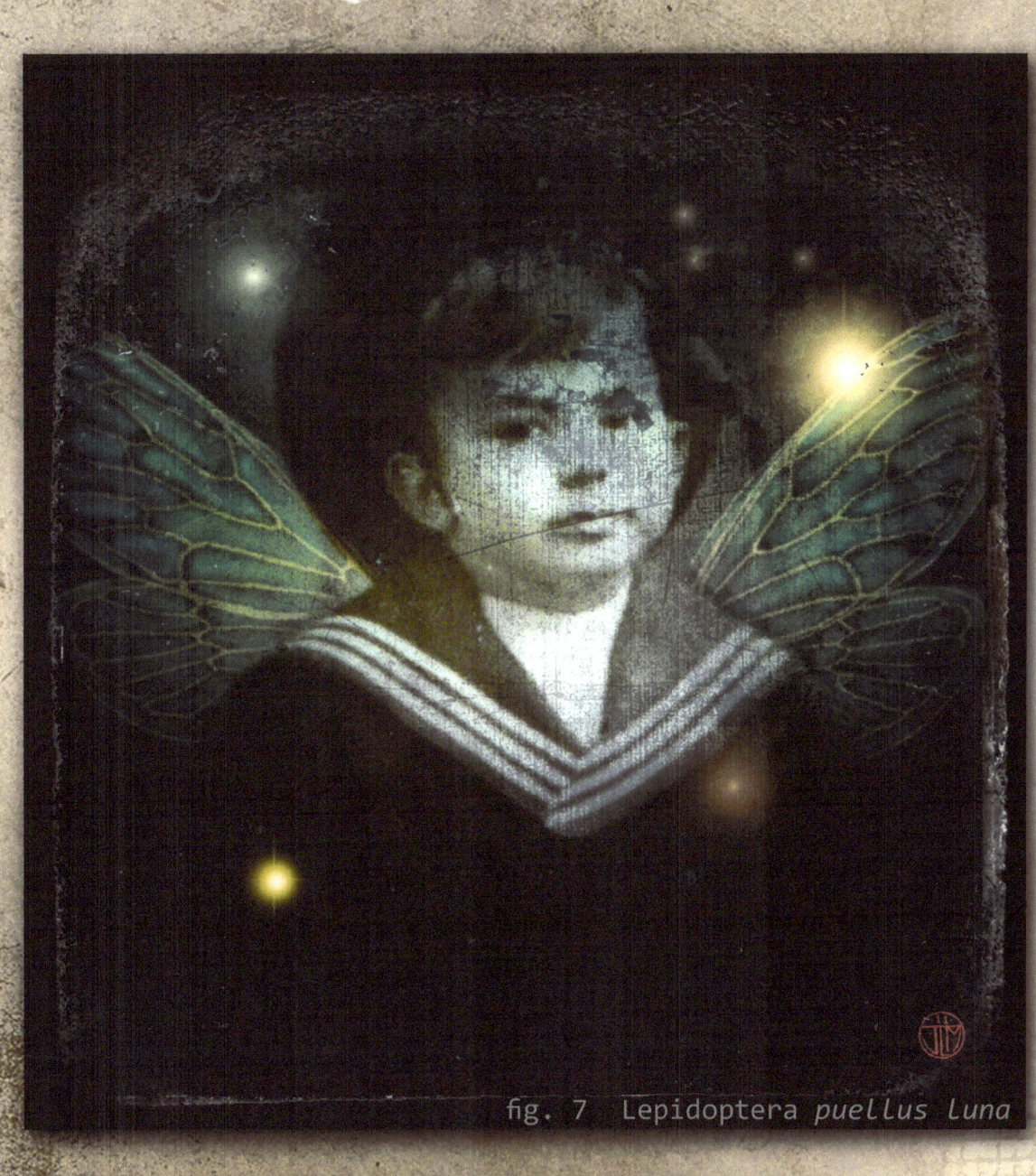

fig. 7 Lepidoptera *puellus luna*

Mothboy.

One of the only known surviving photos of a legendary mothboy, a most elusive and rare specimen.

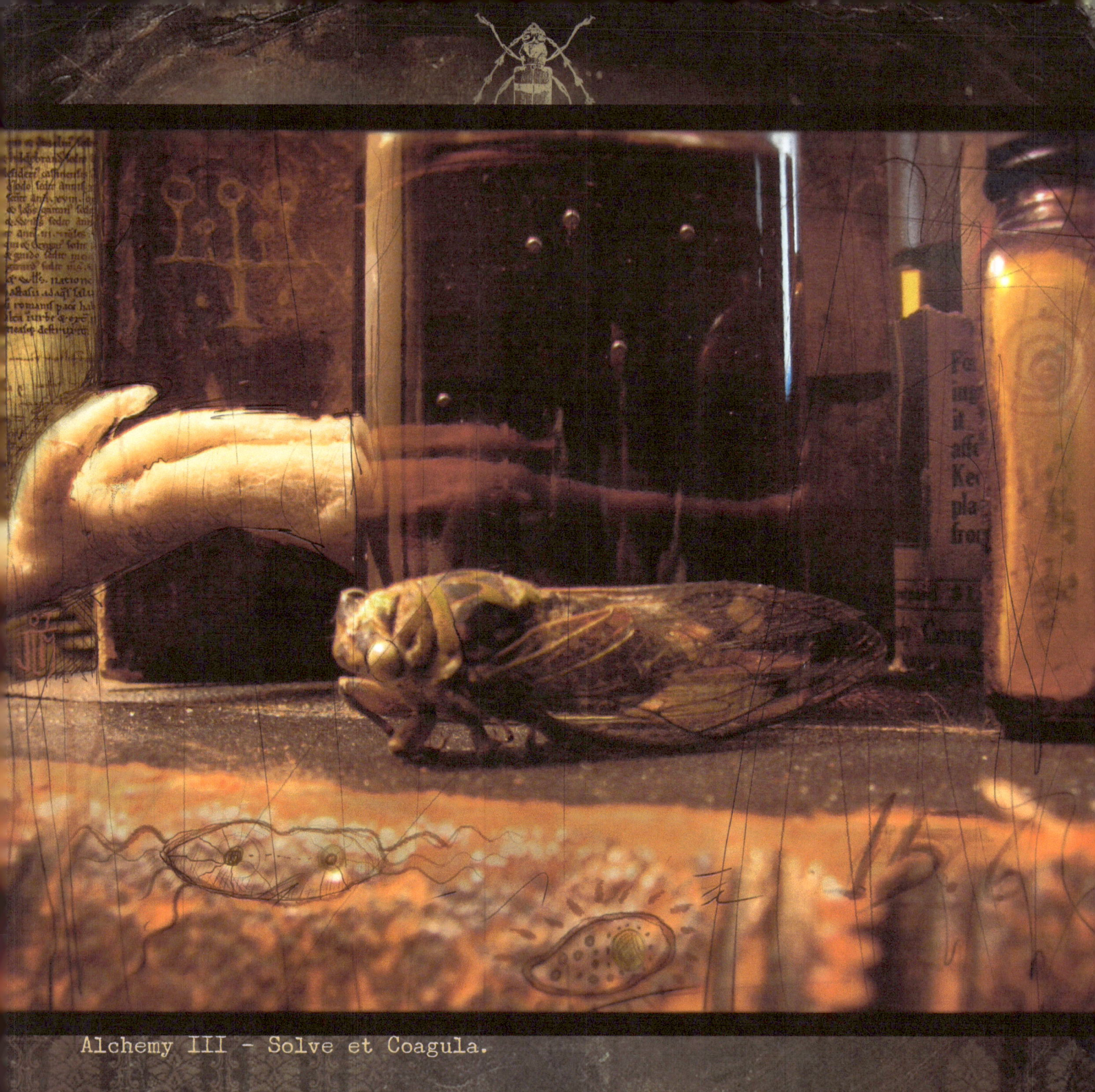

Alchemy III — Solve et Coagula.

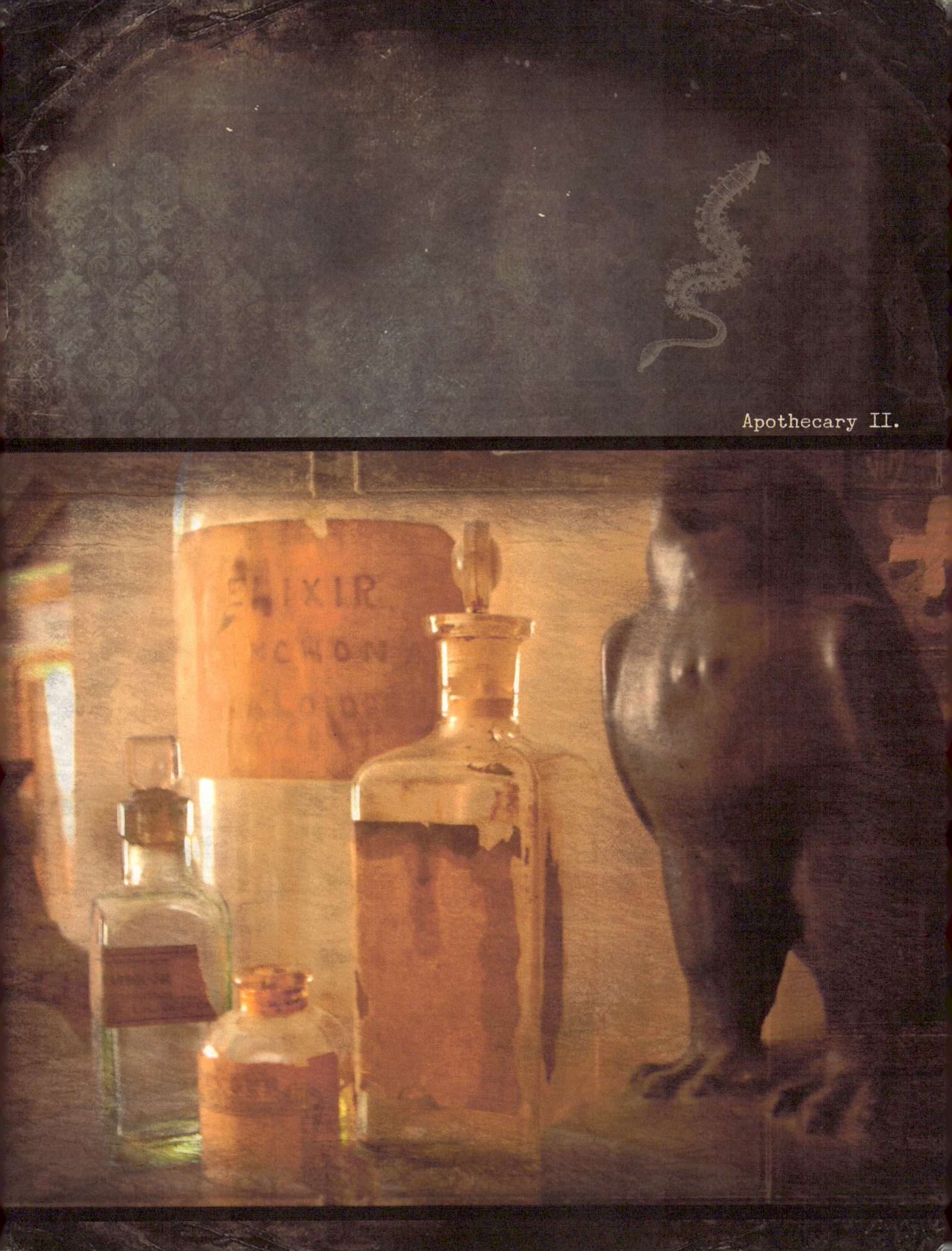

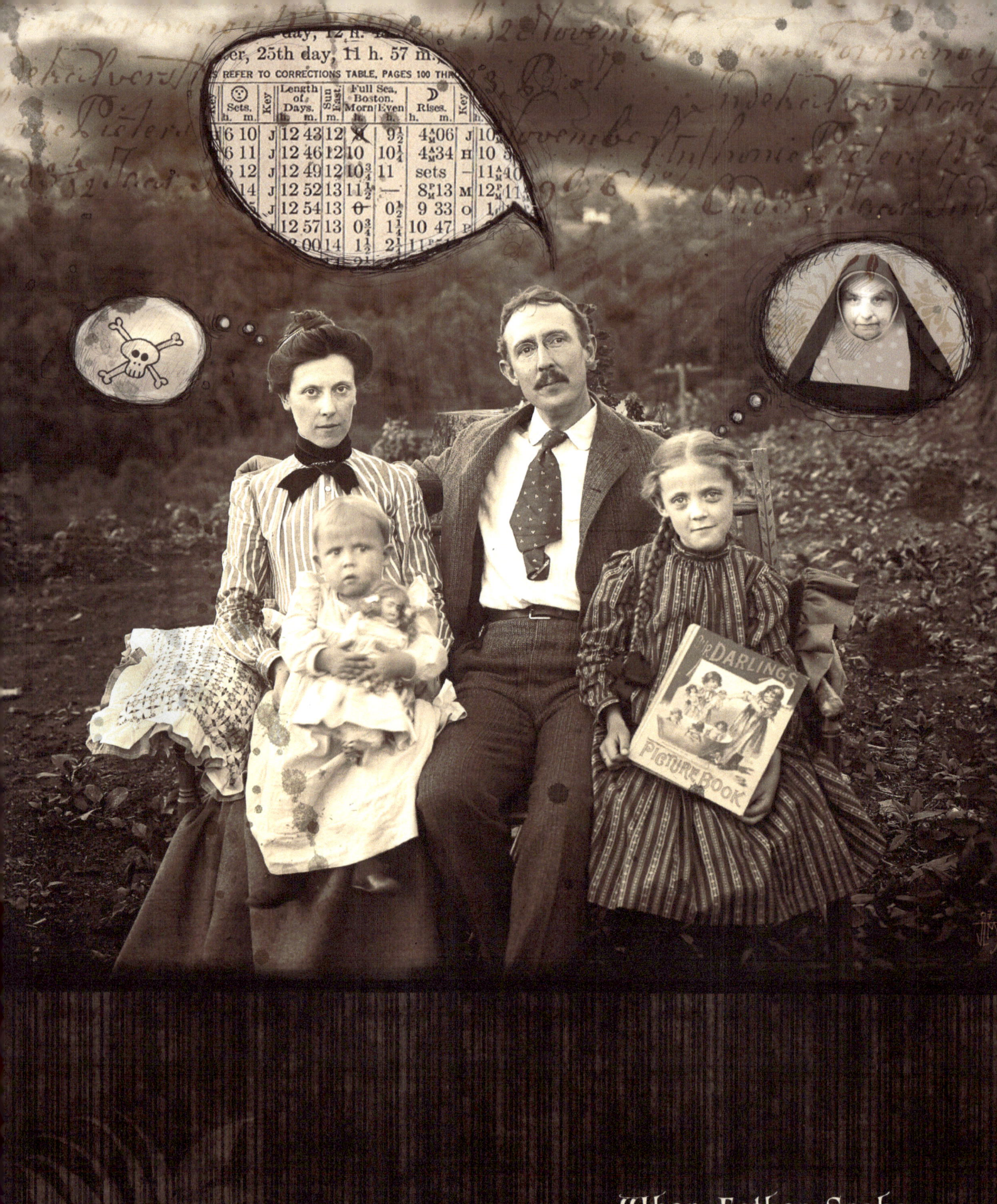

When Father Spoke

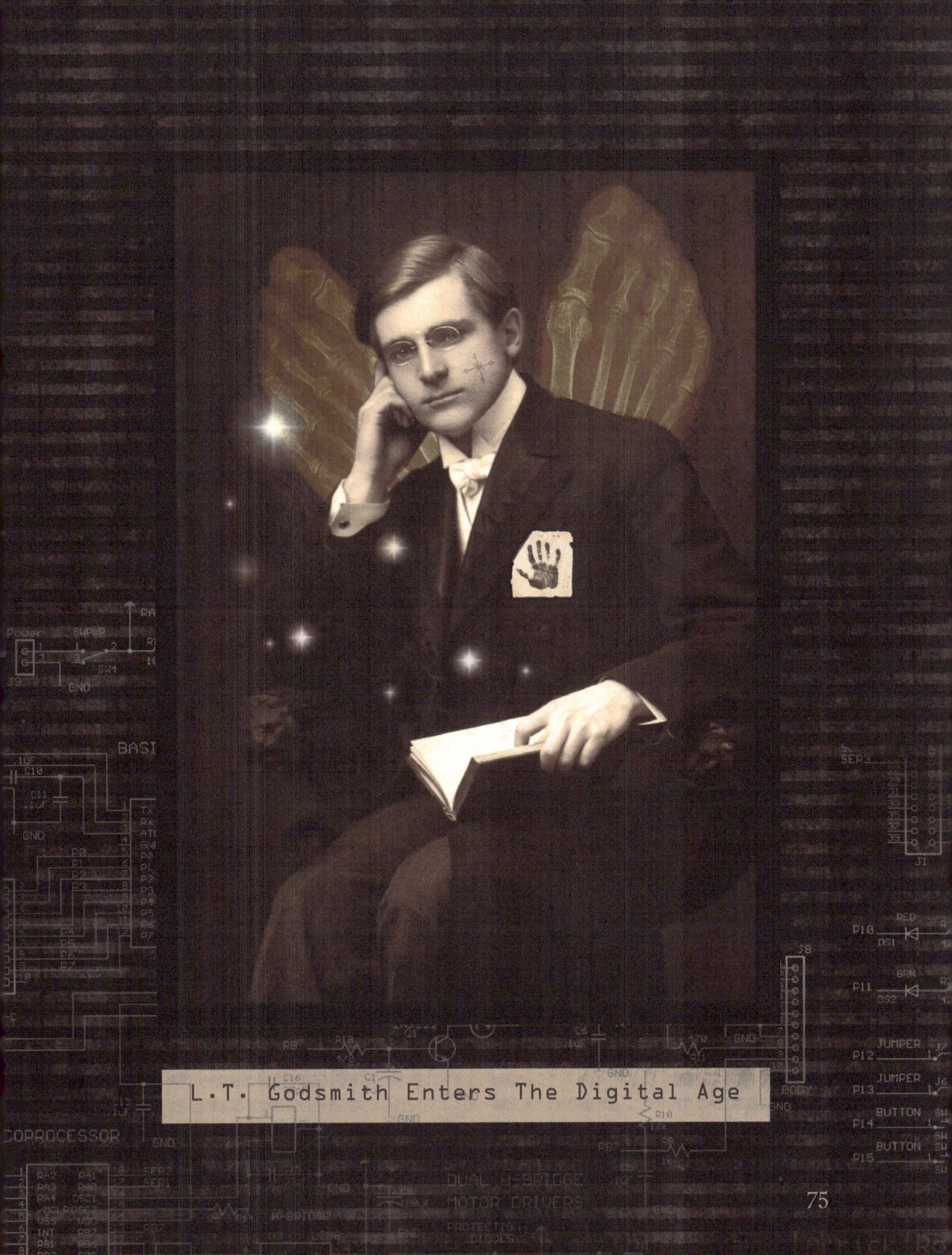

L·T· Godsmith Enters The Digital Age

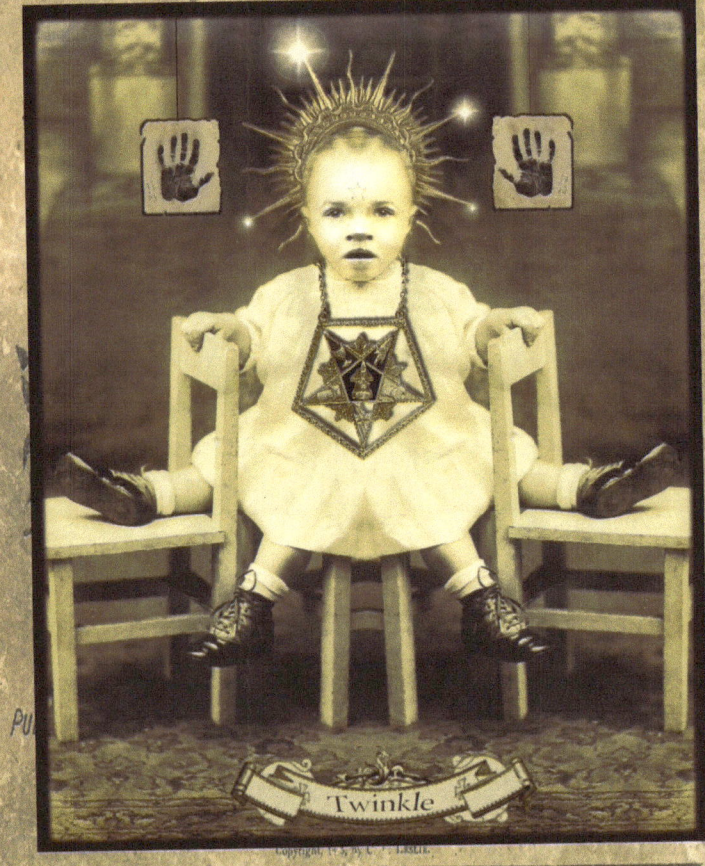

Twinkle

Ṭhē Iṅⱪāṅṭā

Adenine

Thymine

Guanine

Cytosine

the infanta

Though not the next in line for the throne, Twinkle was subject to the intensely mean-spirited scrutiny of her public. While being carried through the streets in royal processions she was painfully aware of the snickers, sneers and fingers being pointed her way. Through the air like small daggers floated such hateful cries as, "Mutant!" "Inbred!" And even "Monster!"

Though life would prove difficult at first, Twinkle was the kind of child who saw her differences as a gift. Through hard work and an enormous will to succeed, she overcame her would-be handicap only to become the *1911 World Cart Wheeling Champion* at the widely publicized Side Show Olympics held in Rotterdam.

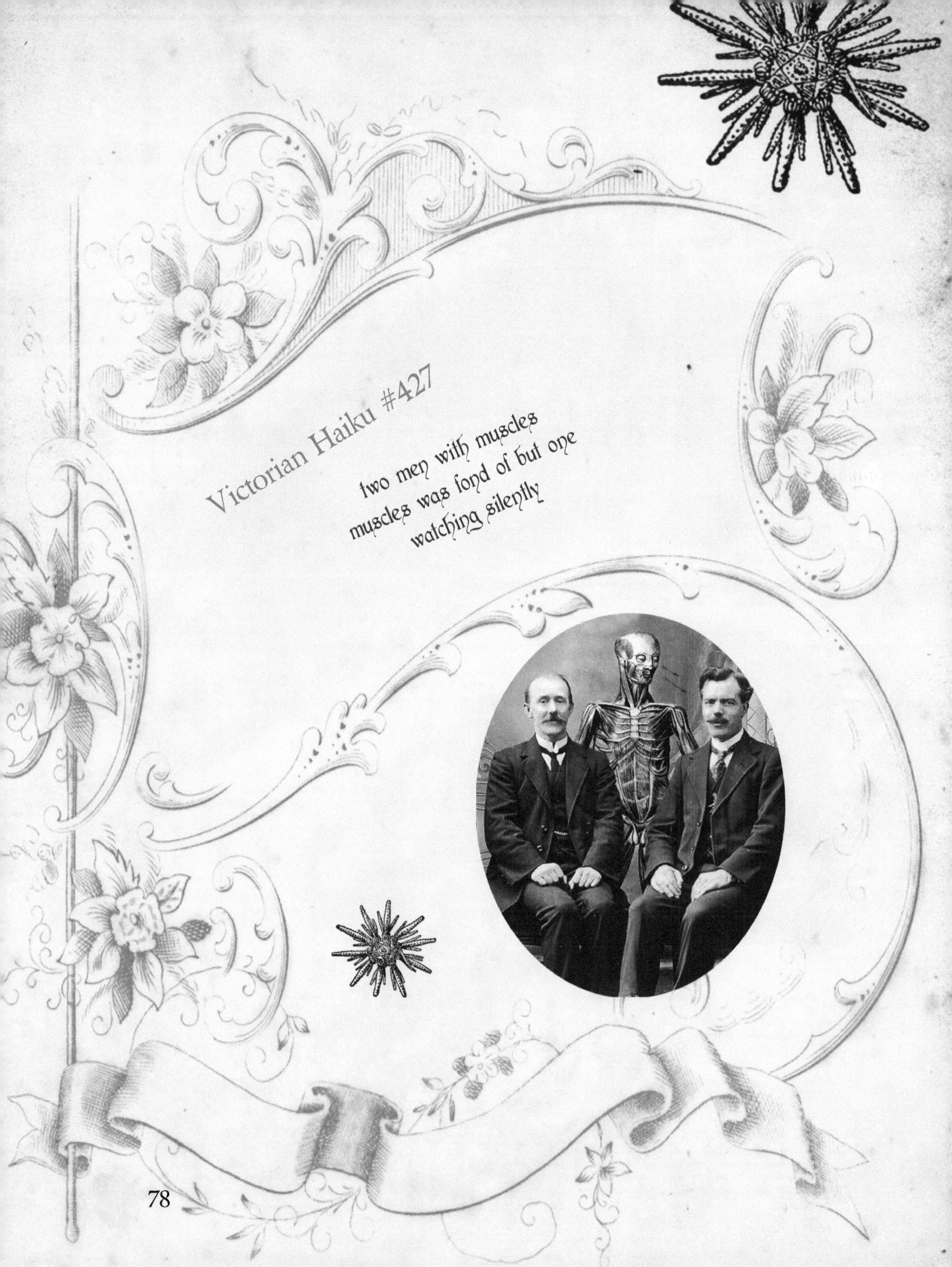

Victorian Haiku #427

two men with muscles
muscles was fond of but one
watching silently

78

Edward and Higgins

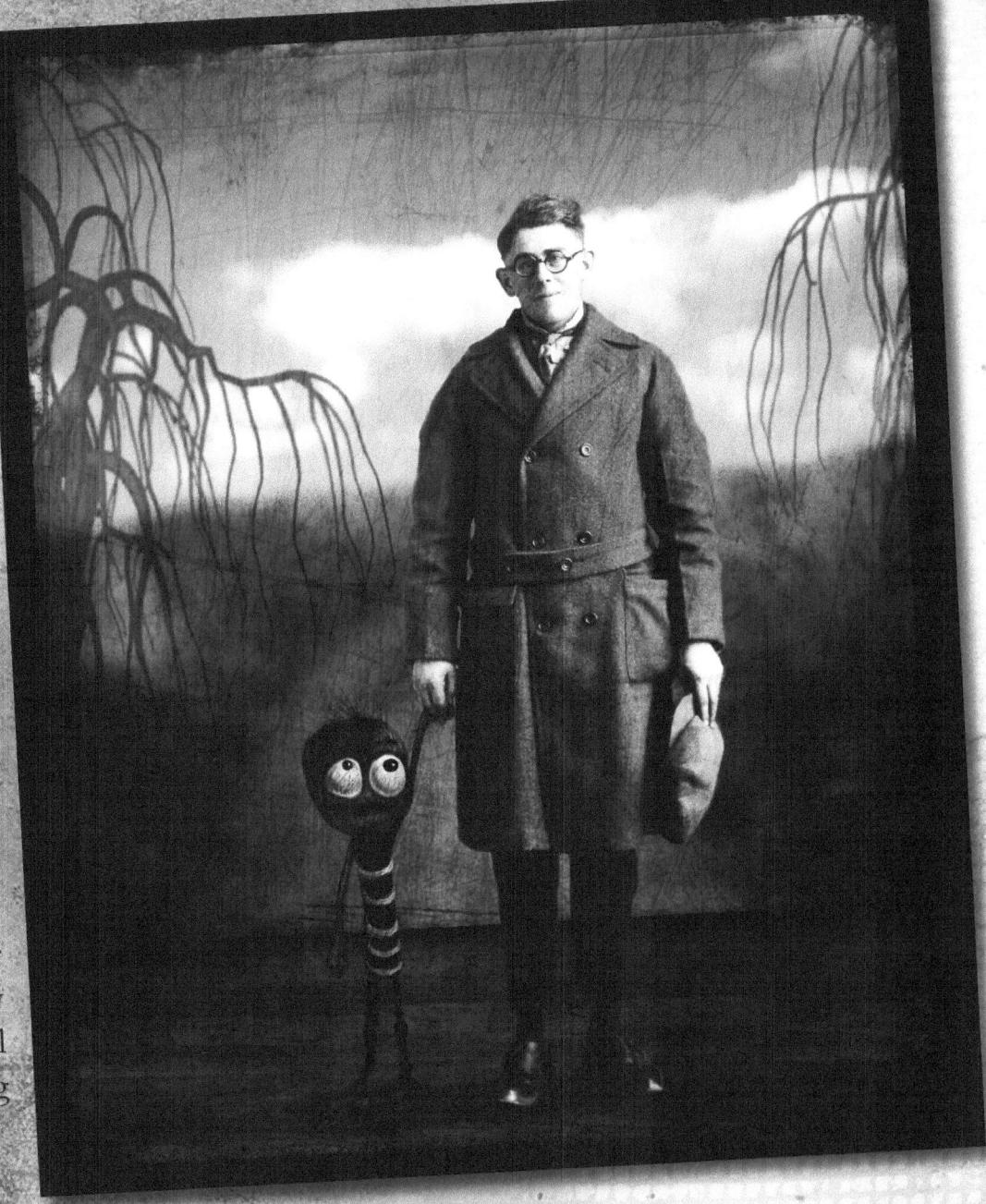

supporter
champion
acquaintance
ally
admirer
booster
associate
accomplice
coadjutor
comrade
fellow
mate
colleague
confederate
friend
partner
chum
companion
consort
helpmate
peer
buddy
pal
dawg

Hold my little hand, tell me a story.

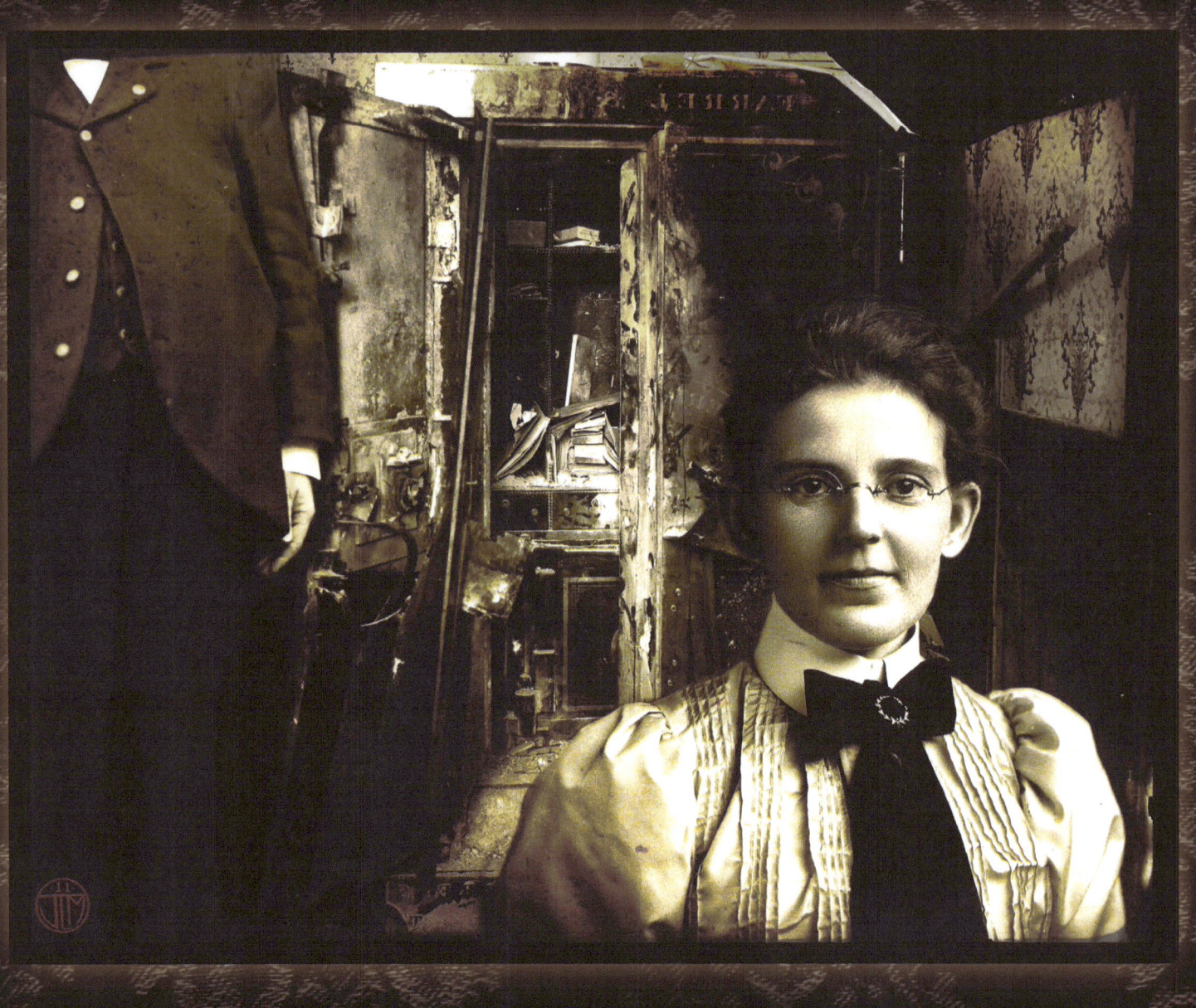

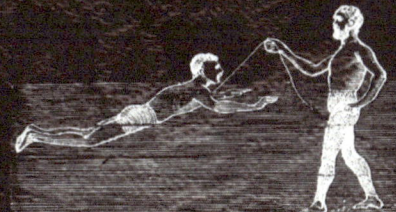

Fig. 6. — Natation à l'aide d'une corde.

The Acceptance of Basil

She was aware every moment
of every day he did not belong in
her home. One day he just walked in the
door and lumbered into a corner uttering
not a single word. She knew he was prone to
destruction—never of her but of things in her
home. Early one morning she was awoken by
a loud explosion. He had blown up the family
safe. Never took a thing from it once the deed
was done. Just stood nearby, not speaking
but looking mildly pleased with himself. She
knew she should ask him leave, but
something felt right about his
presence. In some odd way
he made her
feel content.

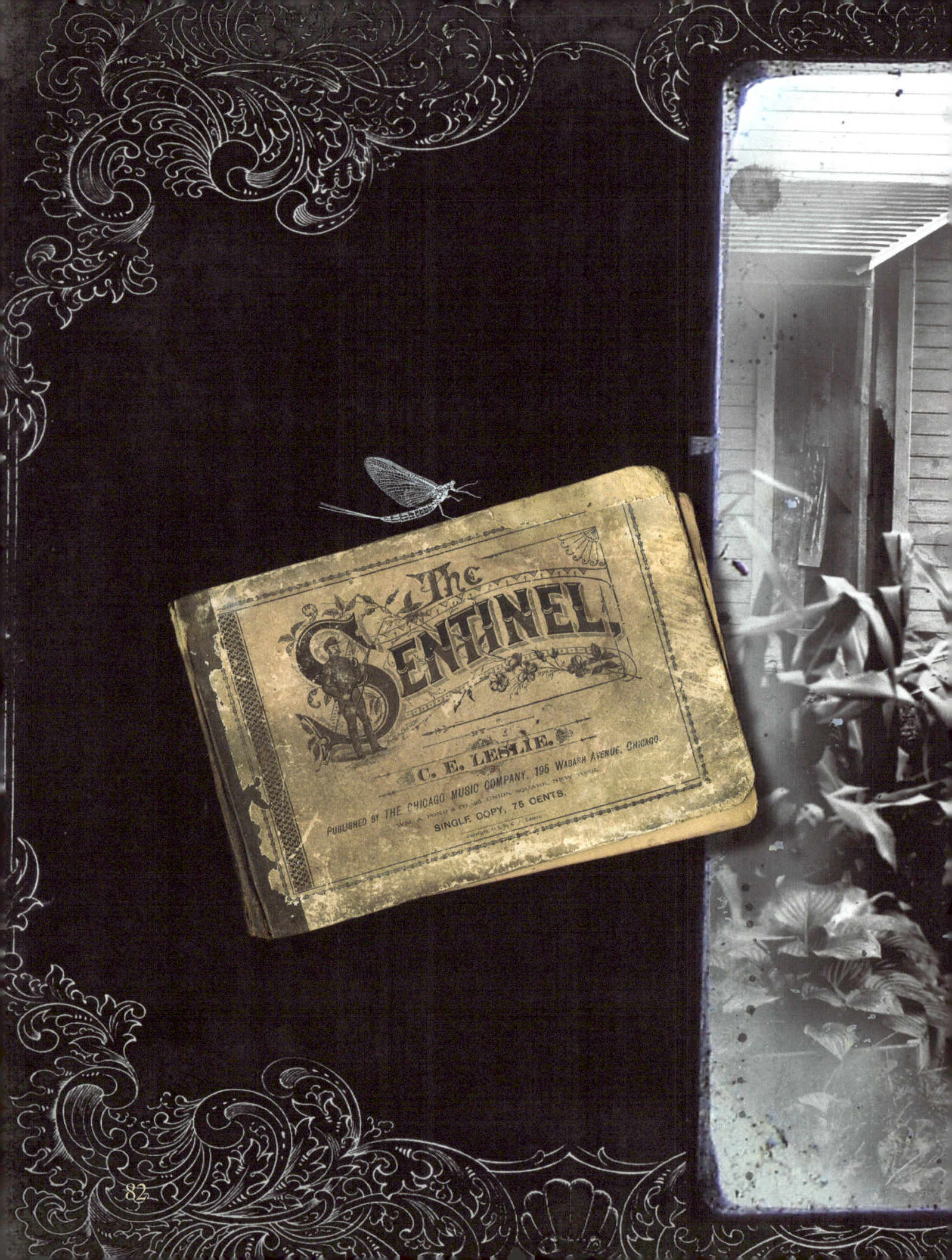

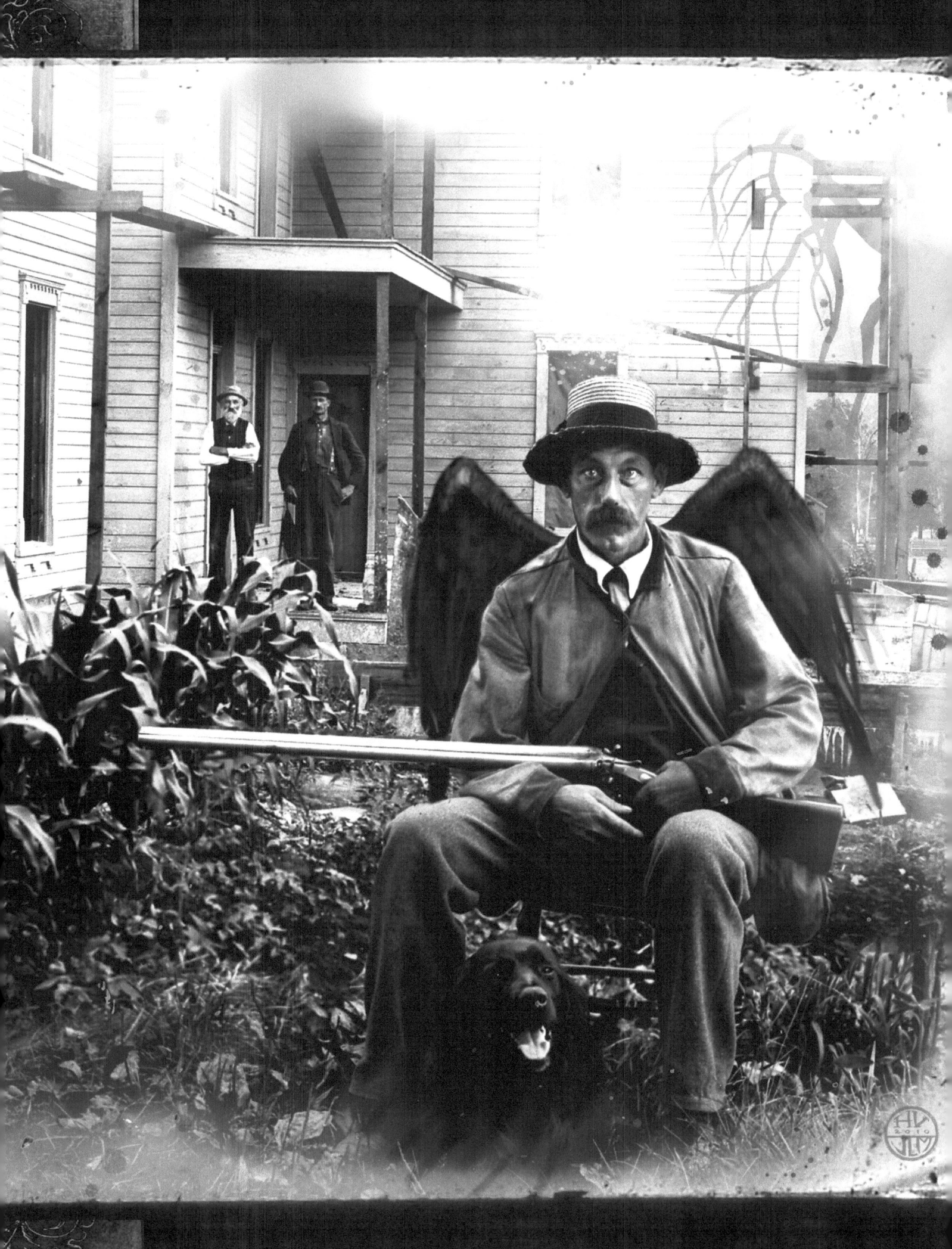

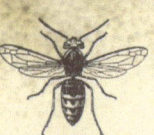

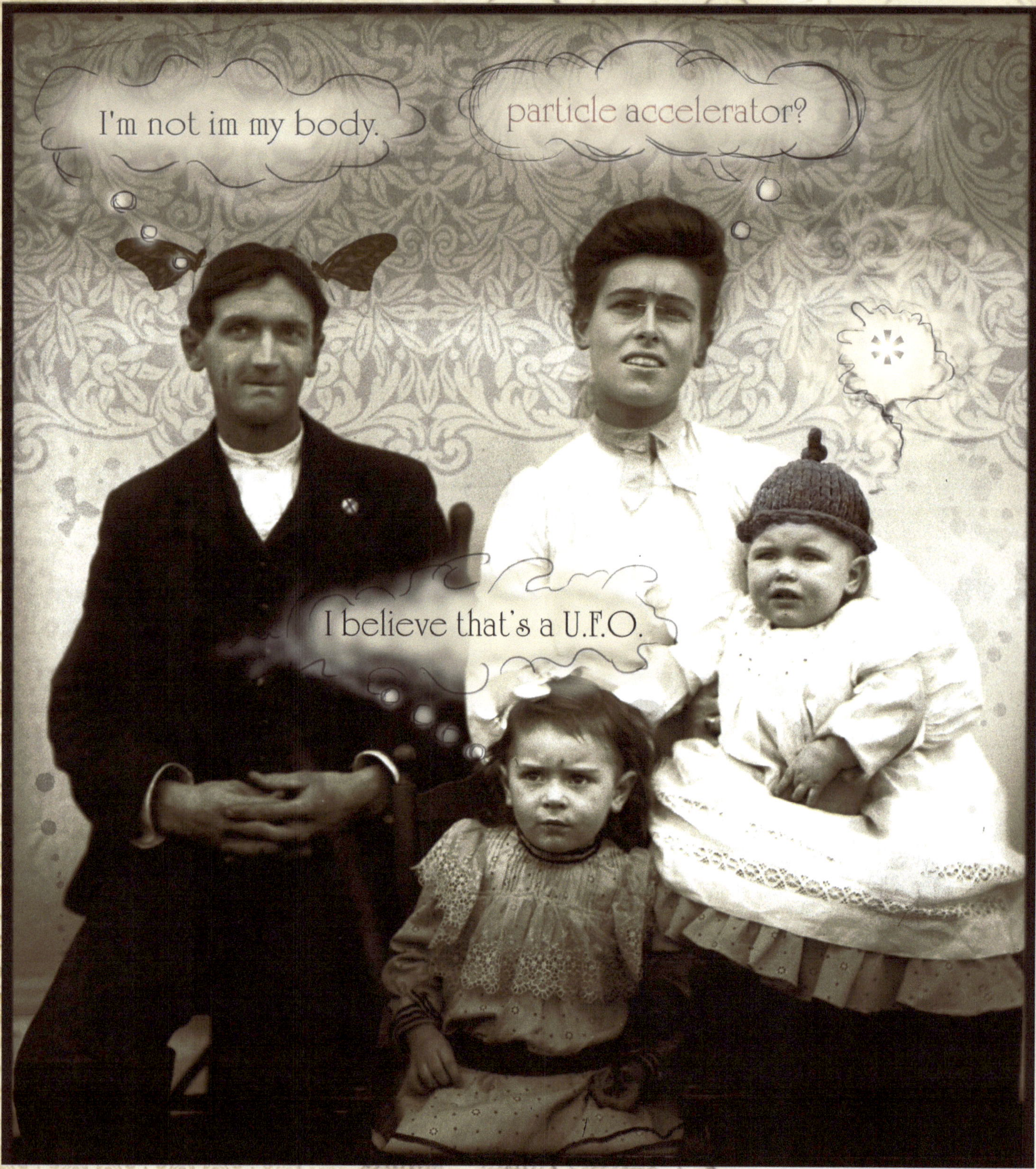

The Crannages Disassociate

Dicht unterhalb der Schulterhöhe befindet sich eine länglich runde, schwach au... ühlte glatte Fläche, an welche sich der eigentliche Arm mit seinem ob... ...knochen, ansetzt. Dieser stellt einen ungemein ... Knochen ... Das ober... mit einer ... damit a... der Sch... die spä... Beweg... weist. aber ... artige... diese ... knoch... Bew... der ... auch ... die ... Kn... bi... A... m...

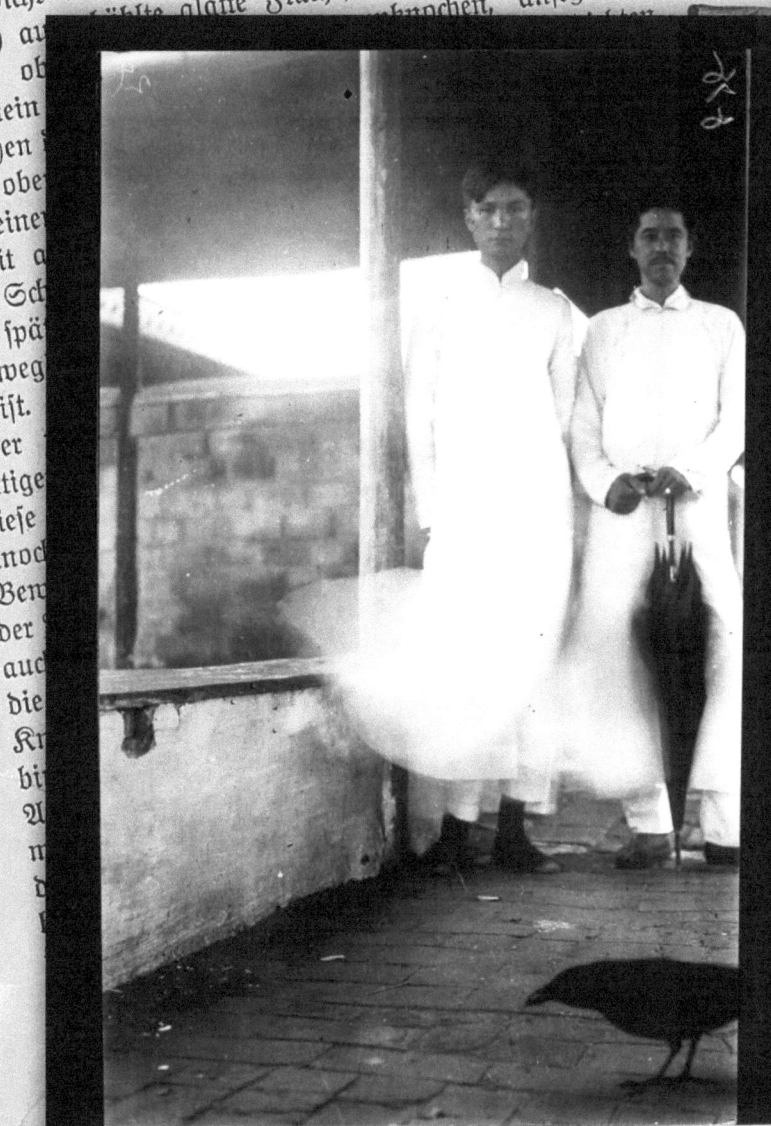

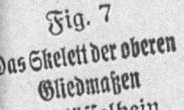

878. Two Chinese who went with me from University to Agricultural School.

Fig. 7

Das Skelett der oberen Gliedmaßen

a Schlüsselbein
b Schulterblatt
c Oberarm-
   knochen
d Elle
e Speiche
f Handwurzel
g Mittelhand-
   knochen
h Daumen
i Finger

Beschäftigungen ... Enden von Elle und Speiche die bei... g... die unteren Enden mit dem Oberarm herstellen, so stehen die unteren Enden mit der Handwurzel in Verbindung. Diese besteht aus sieben einzelnen Knochen, die in zwei Querreihen vor dem Vorderarm angeordnet sind. Ihnen schließt sich die Mittelhand an, und diese wieder trägt die Finger.

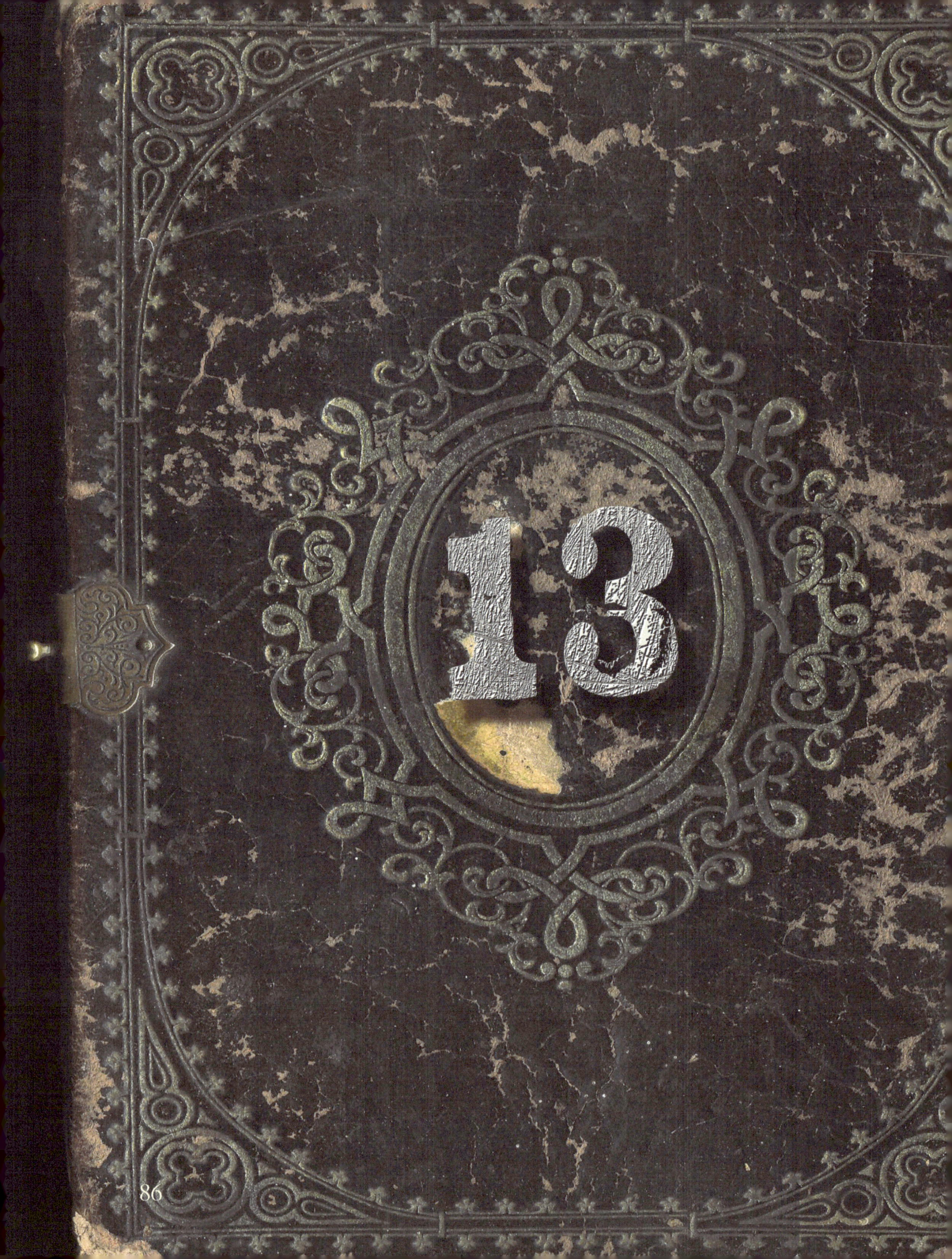

faculties to the Animal, the Emotional to the Criminal, the Volitive to the Enfeebling. It is not essential to discover in the nerve-substance the precise power from which an impulse originates. We may reasonably interpret the functions of the brain, and yet be unable to disclose the duties of any ganglionic corpuscle composing it. We may foretell what each season of the year will bring forth, when we cannot forecast the history of a blade of grass or a single grain of any kind. We may predict the amount of rain for a month, and be unable to prognosticate correctly the

Fig. 70.

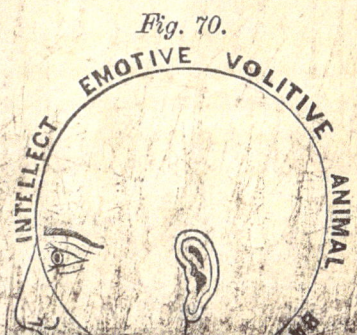

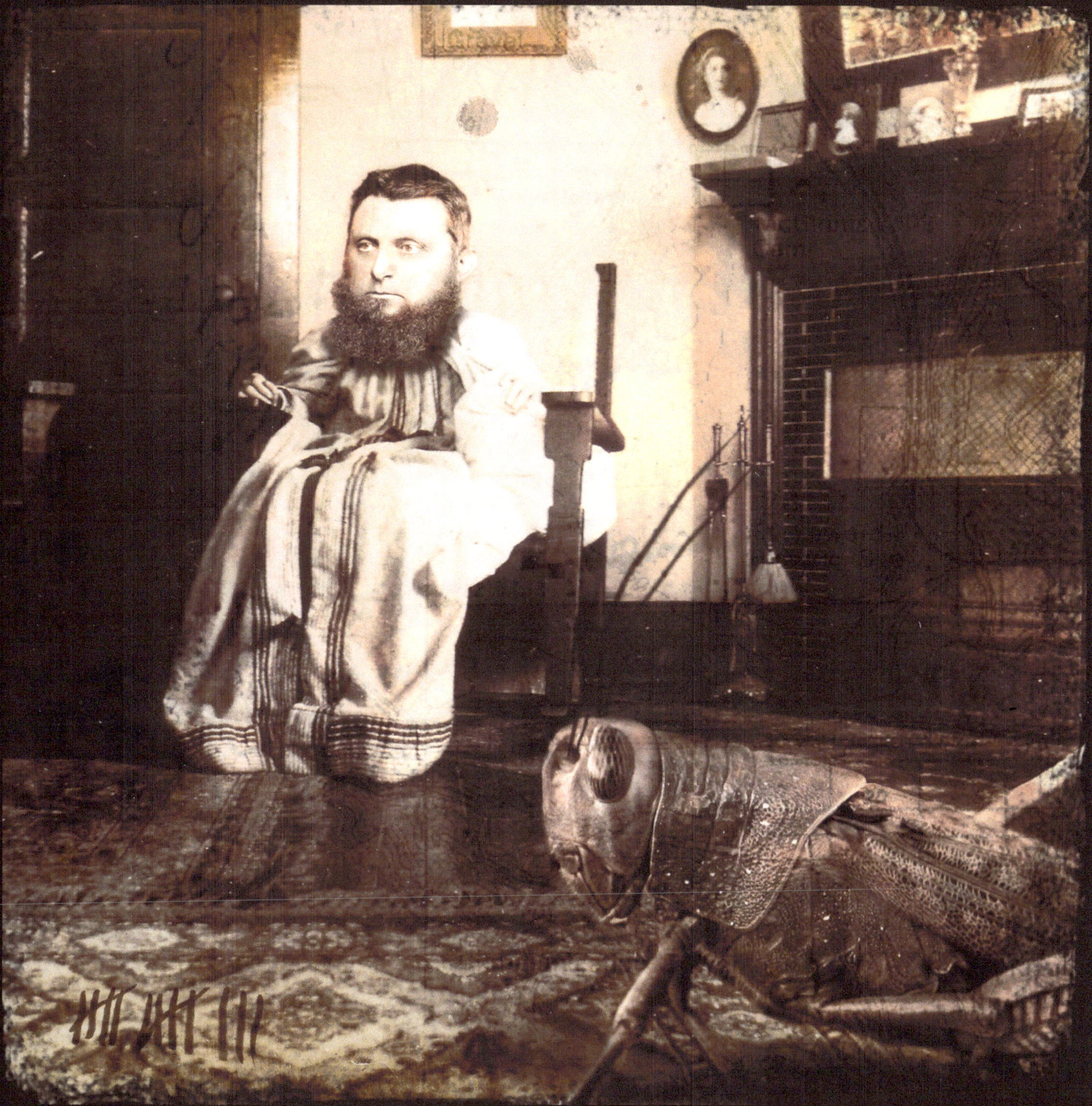

They both questioned their judgement. Why had they allowed this into their home?

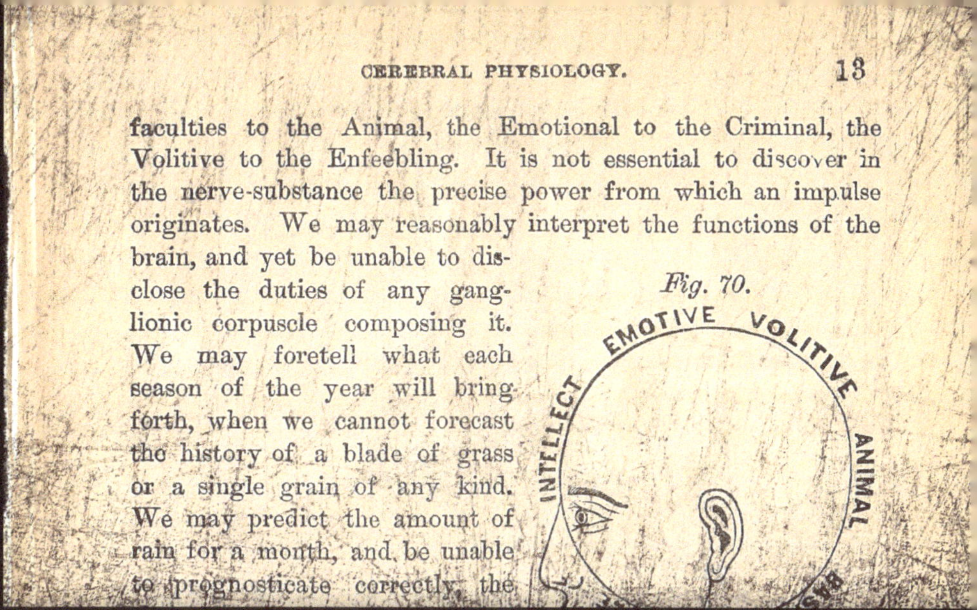

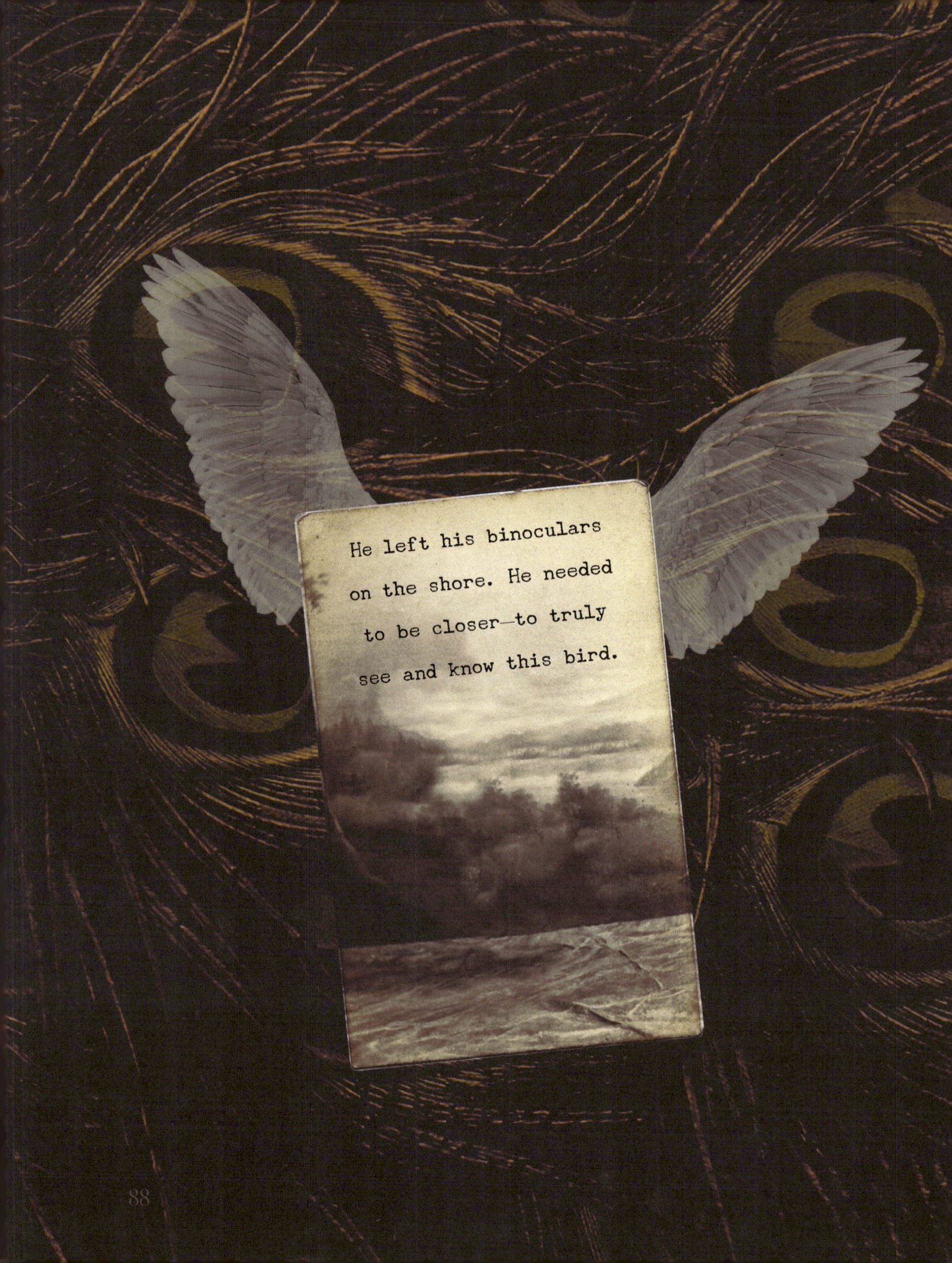

He left his binoculars
on the shore. He needed
to be closer—to truly
see and know this bird.

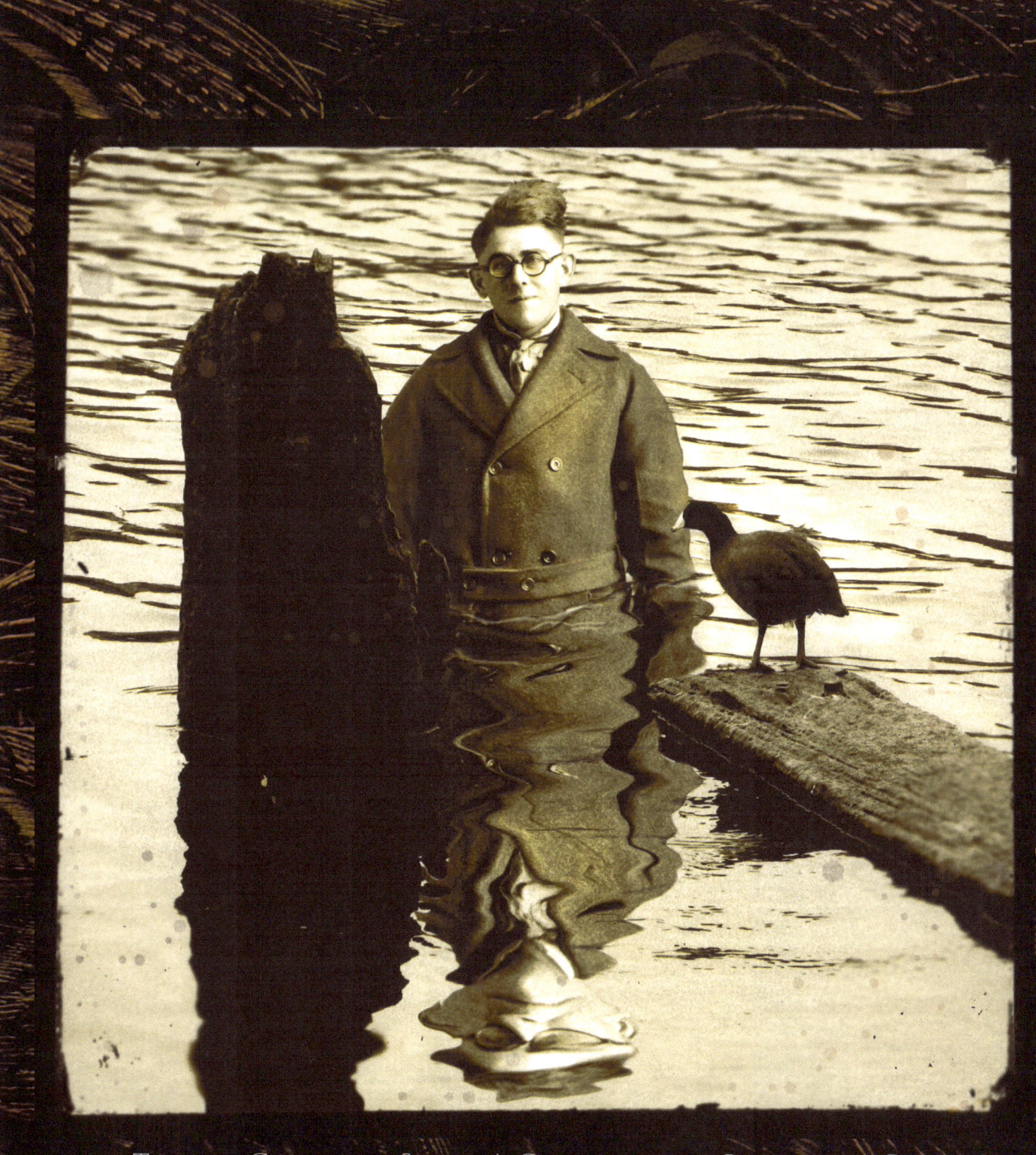

TORKUS GLIBSTEIN SPOTS A COAL-BOTTOM BICRUSTED COOT

'89

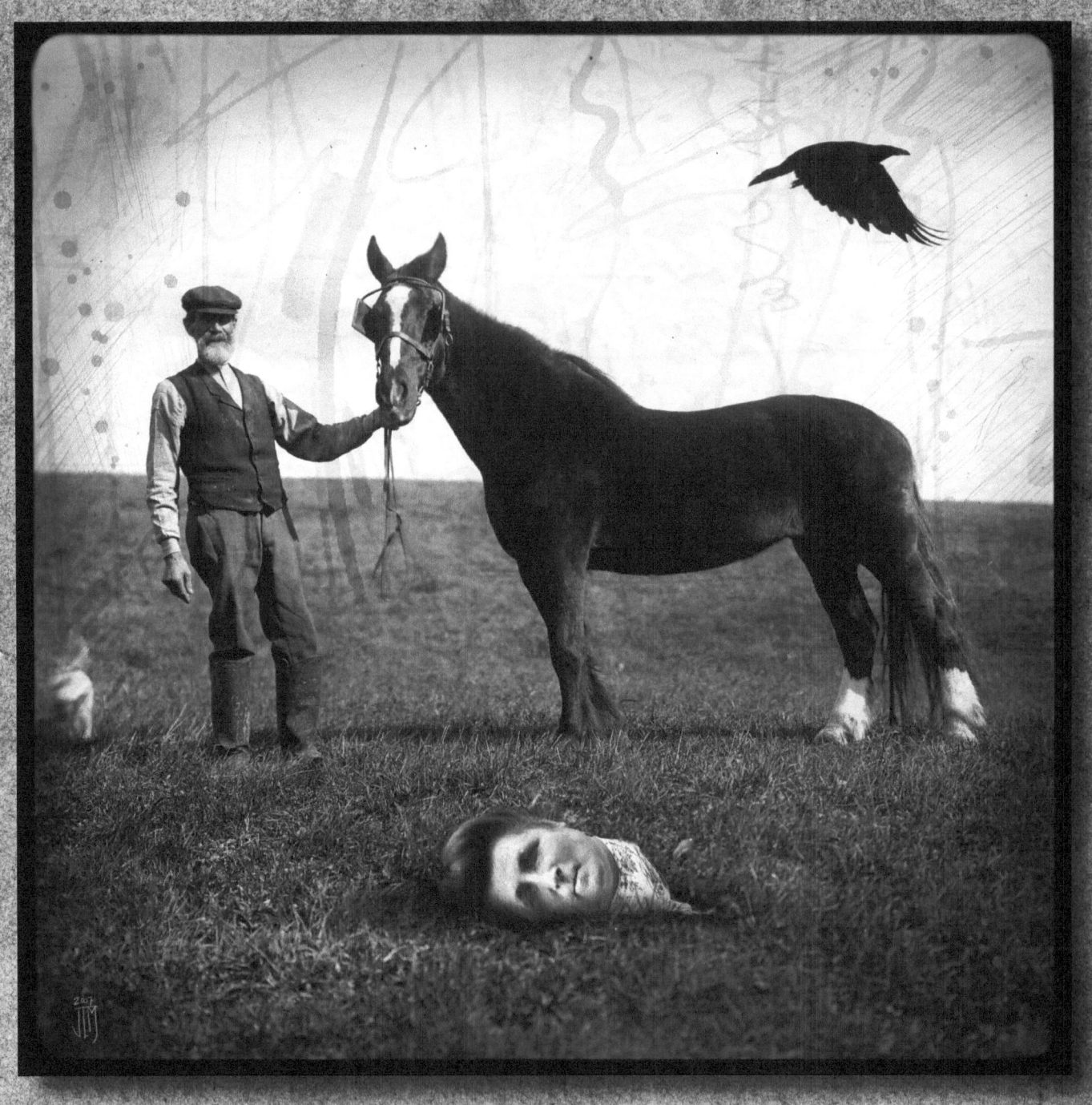

Upon Finding Mrs. Rumplemar

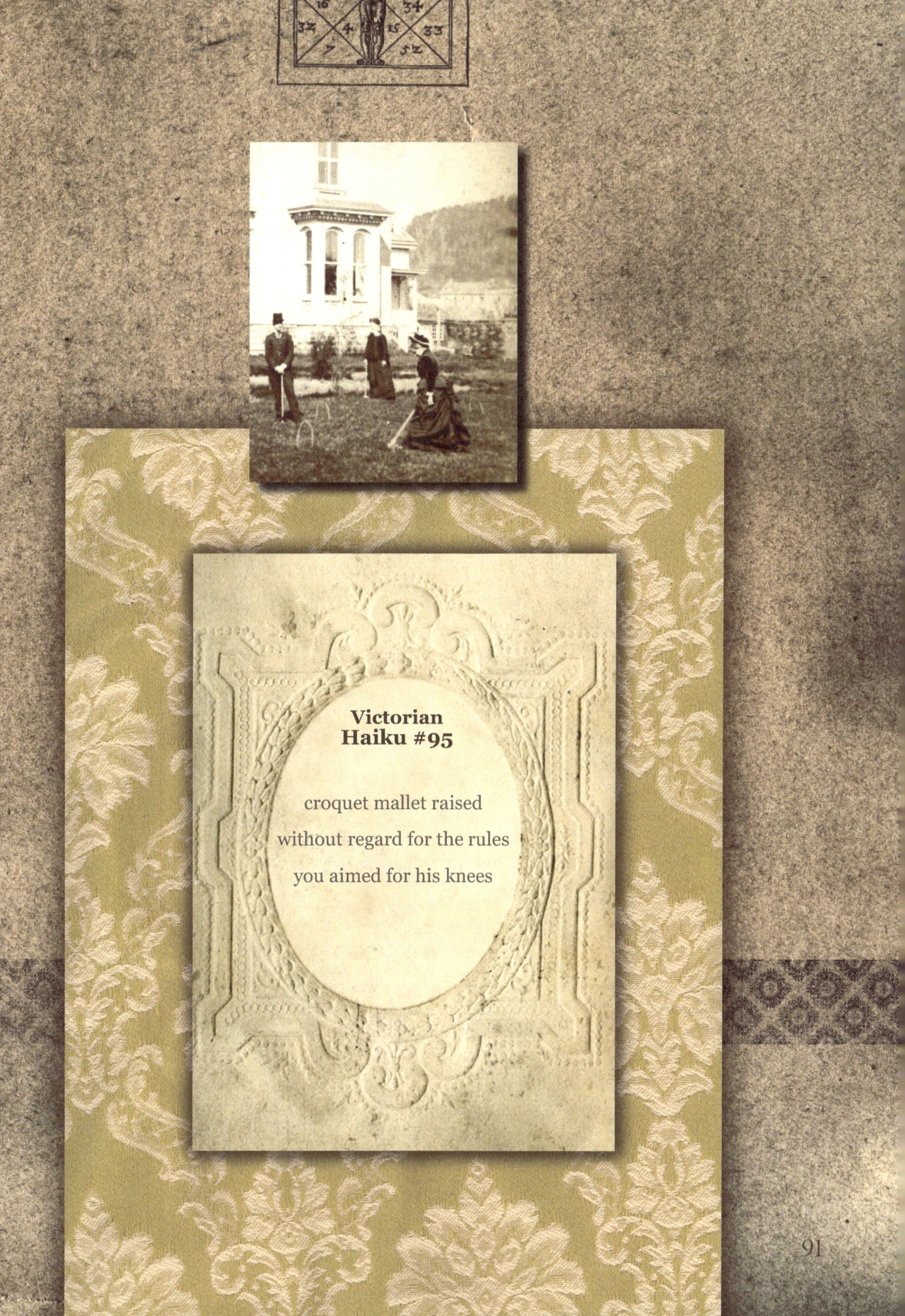

**Victorian
Haiku #95**

croquet mallet raised

without regard for the rules

you aimed for his knees

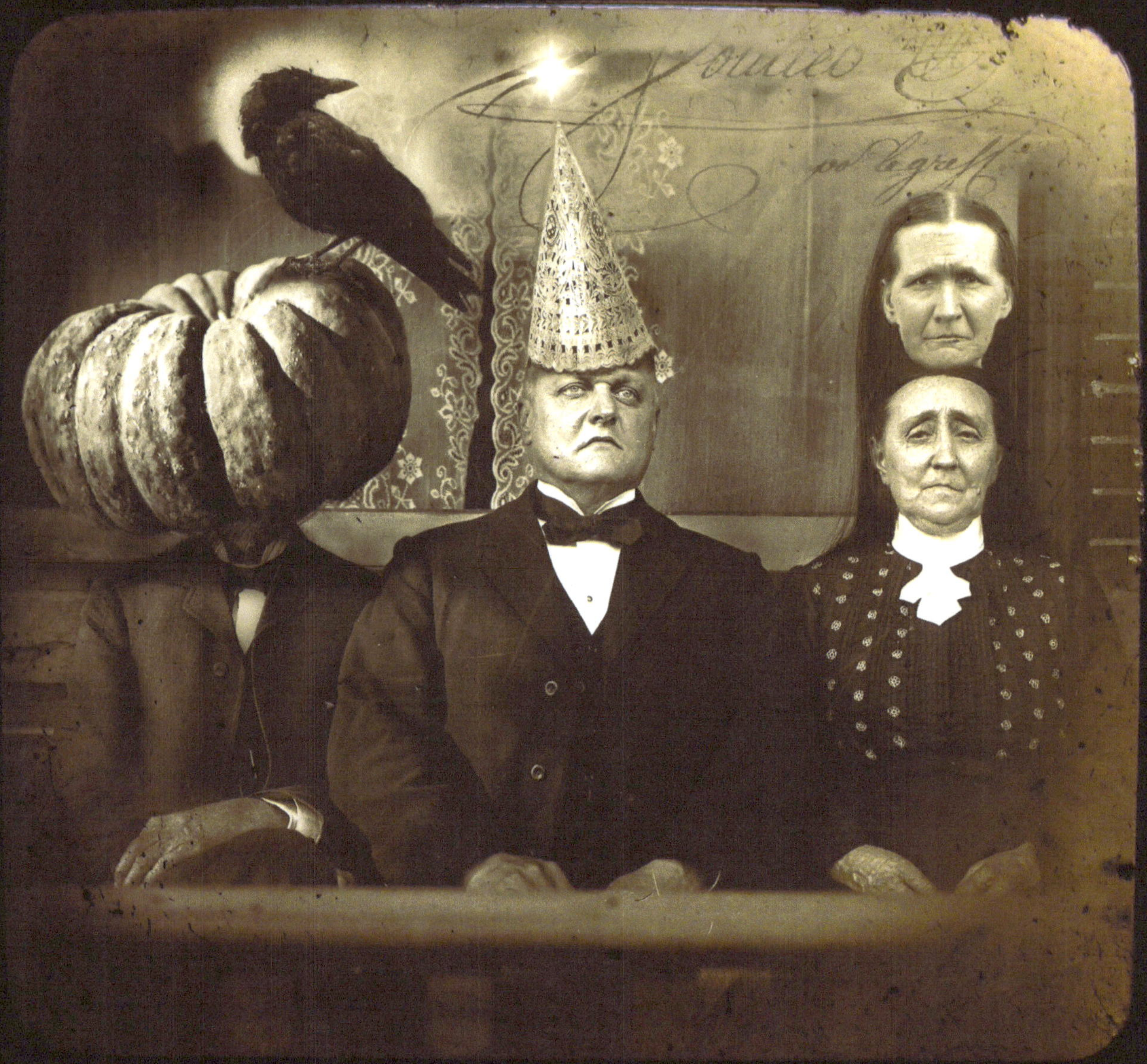

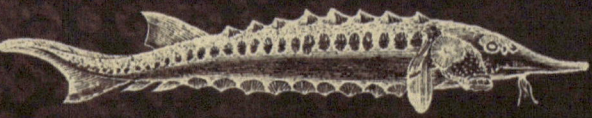

Petit esturgeon (Accipenser ruthenus).

The Wormdumpling Family Portrait
All Hallow's Eve 1873

Though they enjoyed each other's company immensely, it was ever so rare that the Wormdumpling siblings left the damp dark of their looming Victorian home on the hill overlooking Melantown and ventured out onto the porch for a portrait. Seemingly, the light of day turned the corners of their mouths down, made their eyes wilt and their general affectation gloomy. It was only in the dark, with tiny photons of light slipping sneakily through the shades to give shape to their otherwise amorphous forms, that they felt most alive and yes— happy.

From left to right we see Glum, with his pet raven, looking not the least embarrassed by the peculiar shape of his head, General Bilge, the eldest, who insisted always on fashioning a paper doily into a head piece, and lastly the conjoined Eldabee (bottom) and Darnia (top), sisters but never quite friends.

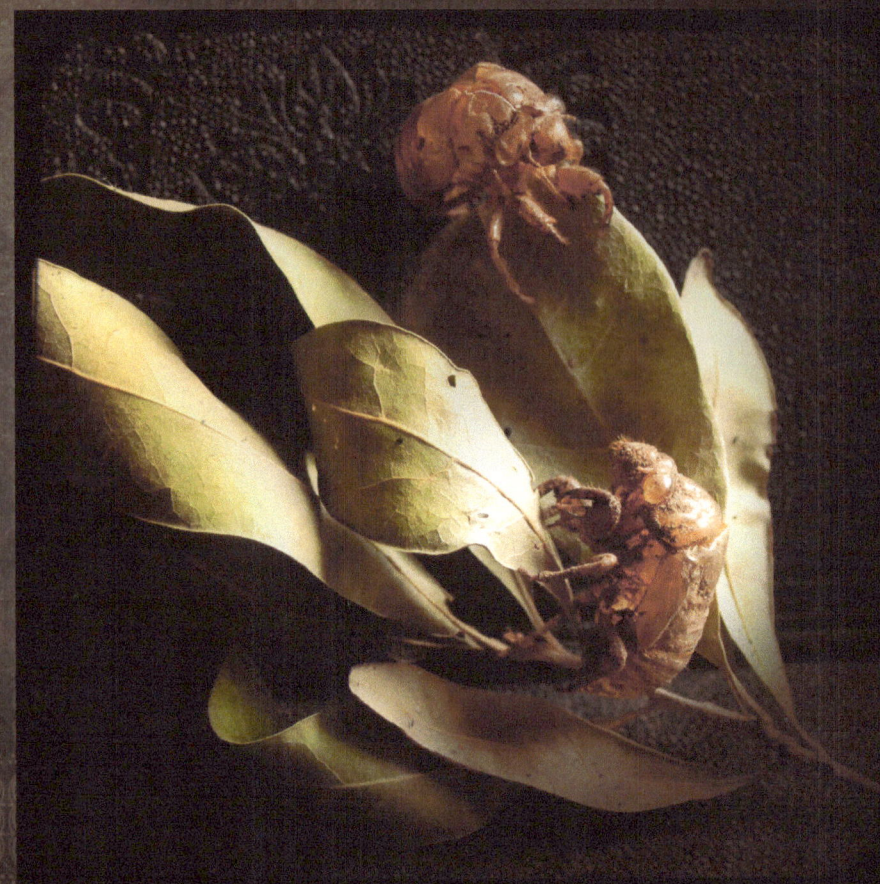

Exoskeletons.

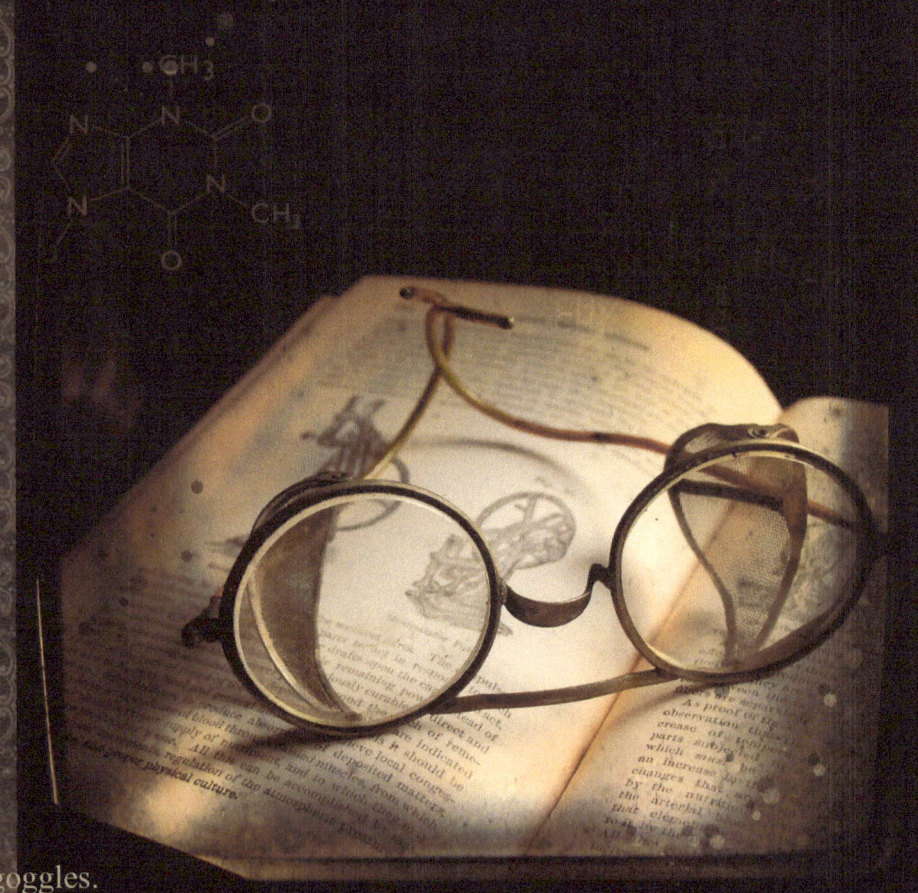

Science goggles.

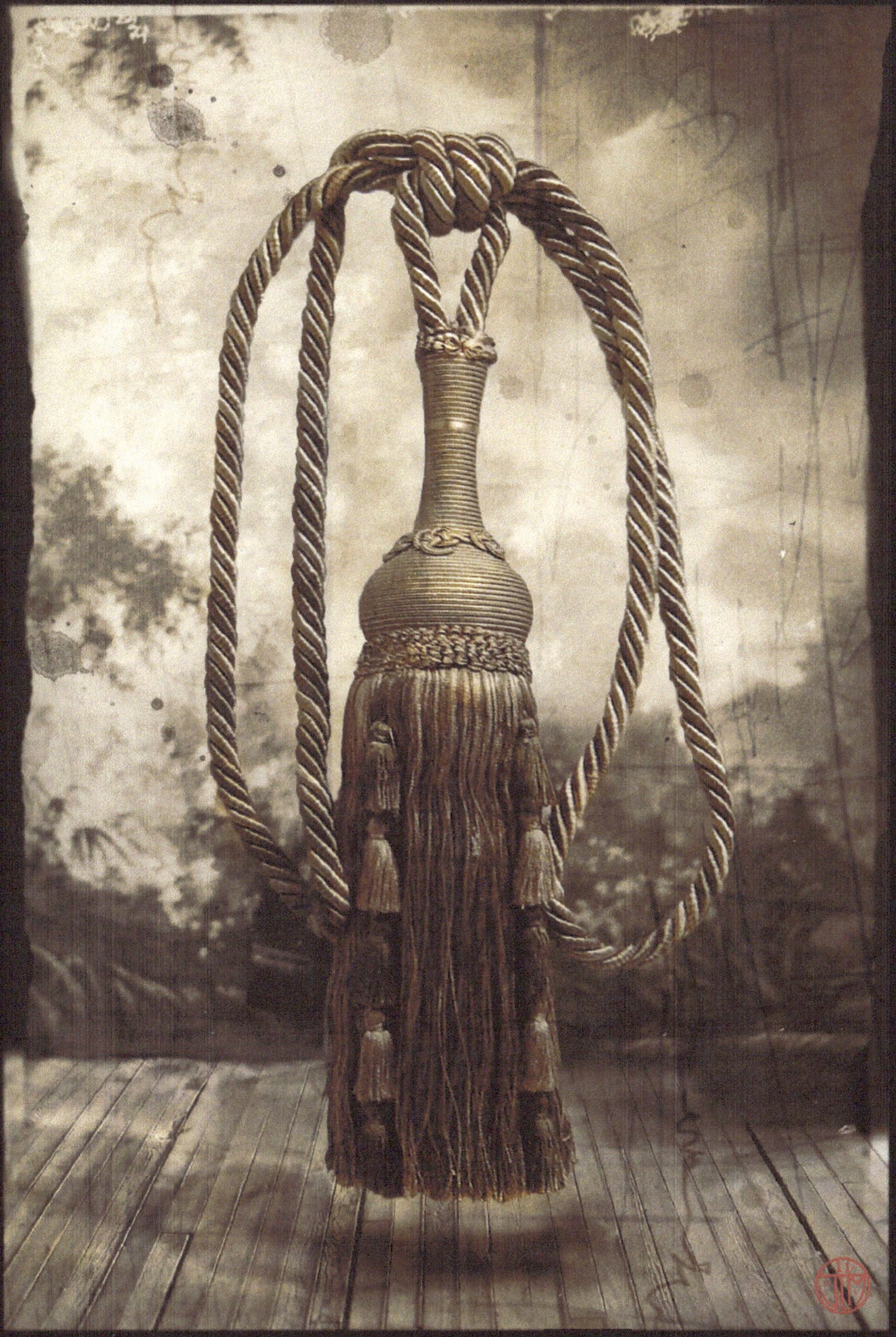

Les Passementeries Horribles

[a tribute to Edward Gorey]

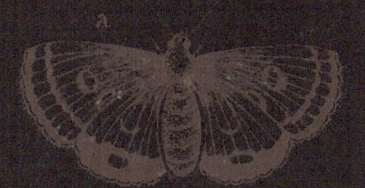

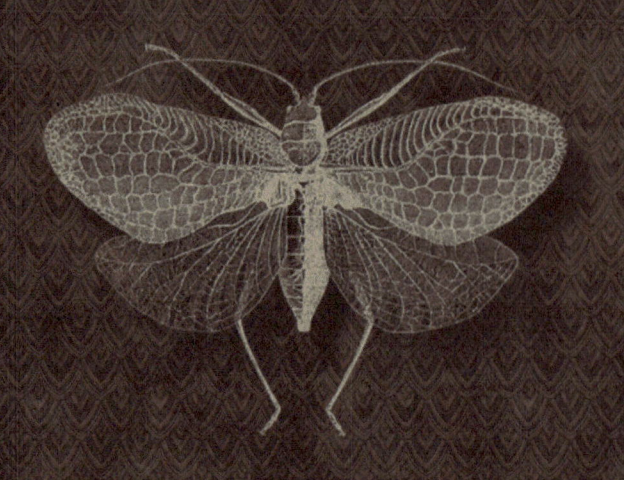

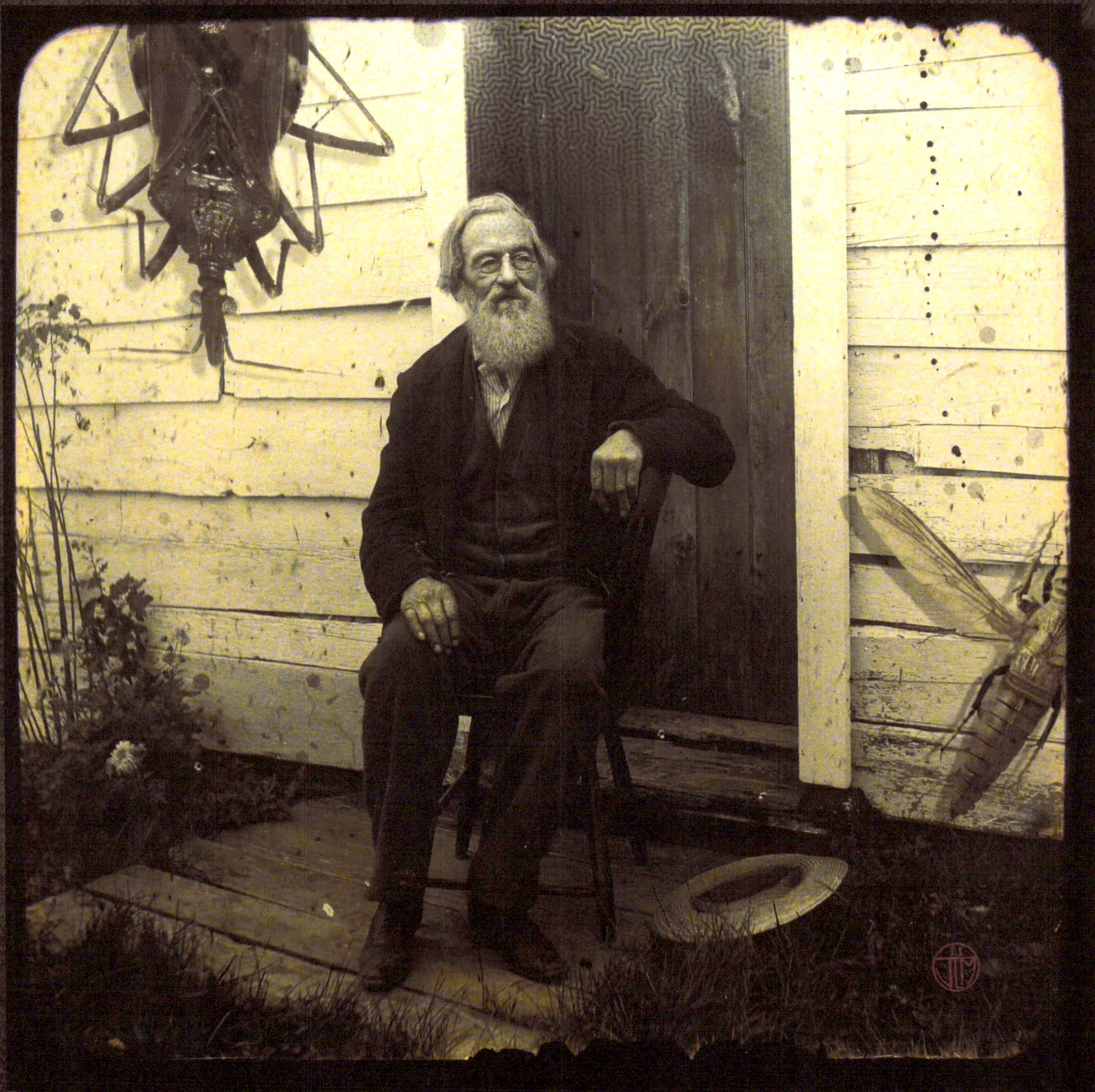

Tobias Waddlecrock Enjoys
The Out Of Doors

It had been a long, hot summer, and now finally, the weather had shifted. Tobias was able to sit outside in his wool suit and feel almost comfortable. With this change in the weather however, came legions of unreasonably large insects, the cooling air causing them to slow to a somewhat comatose state. They were a bit unsettling yet they kept quietly to themselves. Tobias sat with them, unbothered. If anything, they put him in a calm, meditative mood. All body systems slowing. All of them feeling the passage of time.

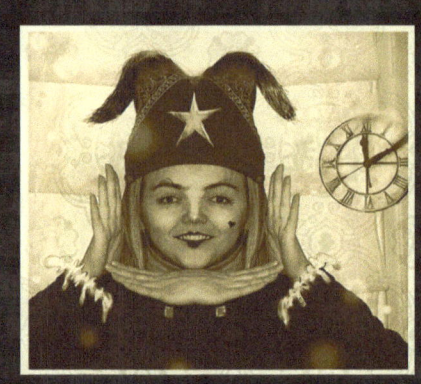

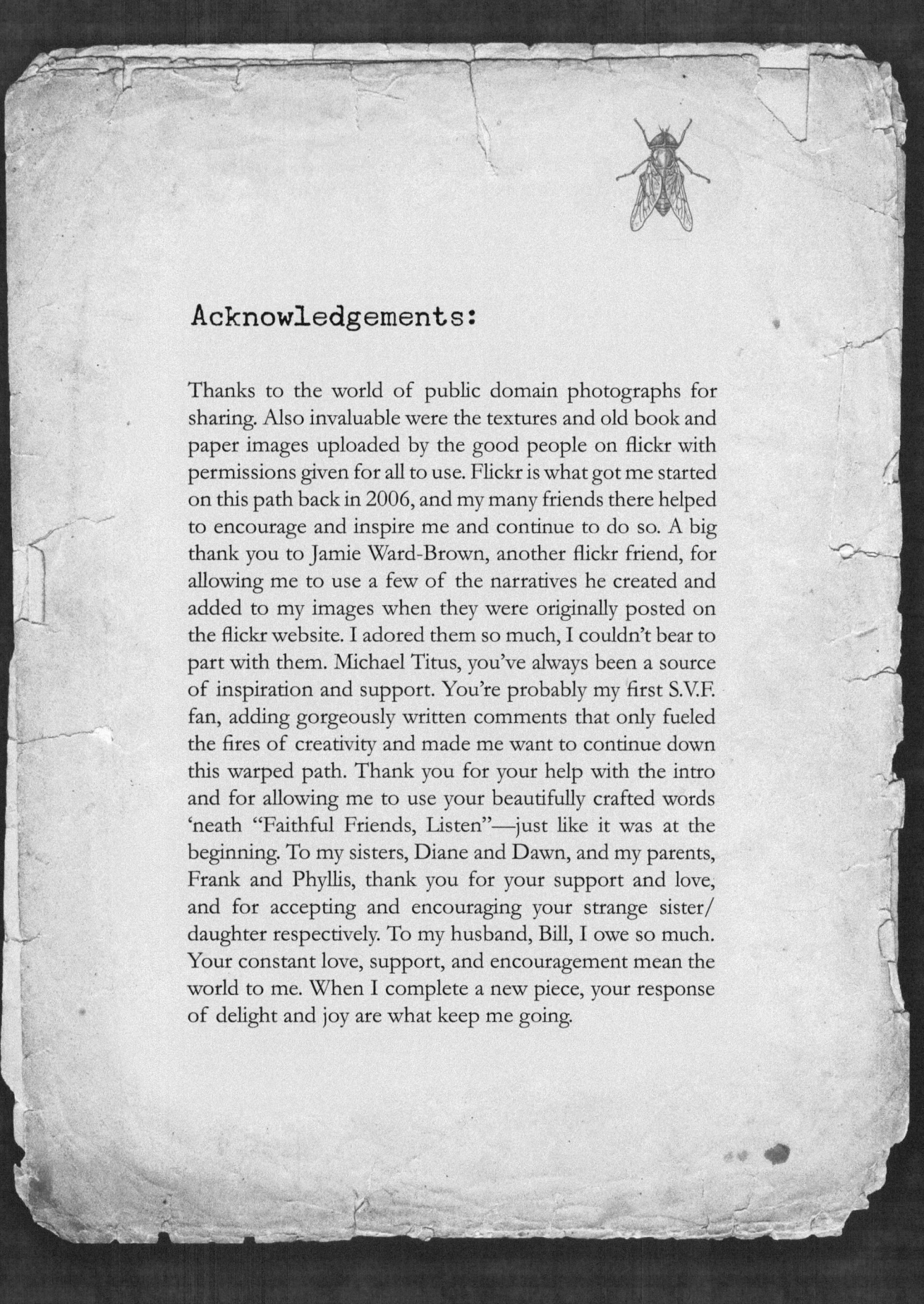

Acknowledgements:

Thanks to the world of public domain photographs for sharing. Also invaluable were the textures and old book and paper images uploaded by the good people on flickr with permissions given for all to use. Flickr is what got me started on this path back in 2006, and my many friends there helped to encourage and inspire me and continue to do so. A big thank you to Jamie Ward-Brown, another flickr friend, for allowing me to use a few of the narratives he created and added to my images when they were originally posted on the flickr website. I adored them so much, I couldn't bear to part with them. Michael Titus, you've always been a source of inspiration and support. You're probably my first S.V.F. fan, adding gorgeously written comments that only fueled the fires of creativity and made me want to continue down this warped path. Thank you for your help with the intro and for allowing me to use your beautifully crafted words 'neath "Faithful Friends, Listen"—just like it was at the beginning. To my sisters, Diane and Dawn, and my parents, Frank and Phyllis, thank you for your support and love, and for accepting and encouraging your strange sister/daughter respectively. To my husband, Bill, I owe so much. Your constant love, support, and encouragement mean the world to me. When I complete a new piece, your response of delight and joy are what keep me going.

About The Author

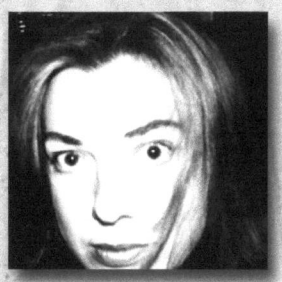

Julie Miller graduated from Tyler School of Art, Temple University with a Bachelor of Fine Arts in painting & art history. After this, because of her passion for the sciences, she went back to school and got a second degree in cytology from Thomas Jefferson University. She uses her visual skills to look at human cells through a microscope in a pathology lab by day, and create artwork in her home studio by night. She is currently working on another book and various other creative projects. She lives in Pennsylvania with her husband and two dogs.

Contact: haggisvitae@gmail.com
Website: HaggisVitae.com
Blog: http://haggisvitae.blogspot.com

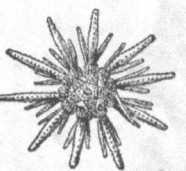

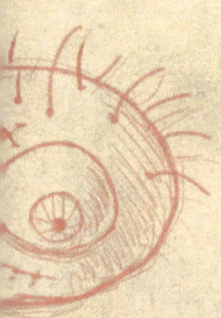

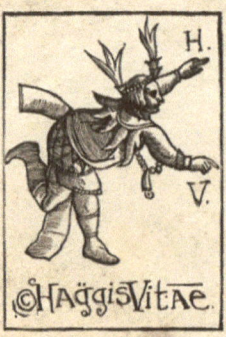

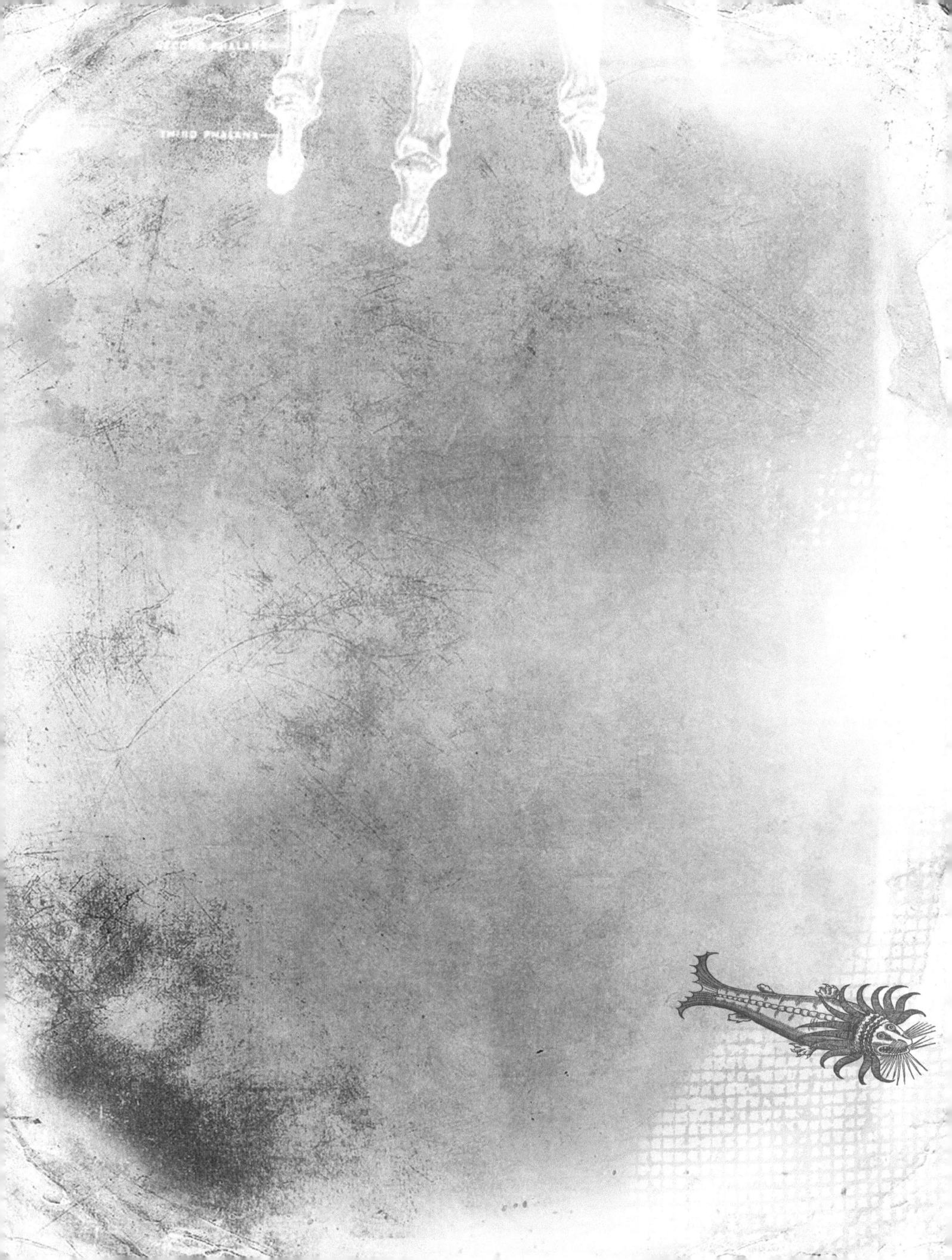